MW01293638

The Saddlebag Gospels

marty & debbie edwards

authorHOUSE®

AuthorHouse™
1663 Liberty Drive
Bloomington, IN 47403
www.authorhouse.com
Phone: 1-800-839-8640

First published by AuthorHouse   4/11/2011

ISBN: 978-1-4567-5233-0 (e)
ISBN: 978-1-4567-5234-7 (dj)
ISBN: 978-1-4567-5235-4 (sc)

Library of Congress Control Number: 2011903721

Printed in the United States of America

Dedication

This book is dedicated to the men and women of
Black Sheep: Harley-Davidsons for Christ motorcycle ministry.

You continue to amaze us, bless us and share with us the vision and mission to take the Gospel of Jesus Christ to all of those who ride.

You are more than friends. You are family!

~Marty & Debbie

Cover Photo by Steve Grace

Table of Contents

Introduction

Since the writing of our first book, "Psalms For Bikers" in 2008, we have had the privilege of adding thousands of miles, unforgettable experiences and more terrific people to our lives. Especially memorable was a trip to Australia in 2009 with a whole new array of sights and sounds as we toured the back-country, rolled along the Gold Coast and took in the richness of the culture. What made it even more memorable for us were the friends that came with us from America and the new friends that we made down under.

Riding motorcycles and the joy it brings continues to draw us in by introducing us to some of the best people we've ever met and challenging us with new adventures around every curve in the road. As we've noted before, bikers are spiritual people. How can we not be when all of our senses are flooded every time we throw a leg over the saddle and get in the wind?

Many of us, however, still do not recognize that there is a God who has made all of this possible. He loves each of us and wants for us to know who He is. In the New Testament, Jesus wanted the people He came in contact with to know more about this One He referred to as the Father. But He recognized that there was a huge disconnect when it came to the average person and their understanding of God. Unfortunately, God had been grossly misrepresented both by the religious establishment and political figures in power at that time. So, in an attempt to change all that, He told a lot of stories that would relate to His listeners. He used common things they would already know about like families, food and livestock that they saw and touched every day. That's why we have the parables which are in essence an earthly and familiar story with a spiritual meaning.

All of the examples He gave have value for us today because Jesus still wants us to understand more about God. In many ways, people are the same as they were back then and in our heart of hearts we have similar hopes, dreams and fears that were identified by Him as He walked the Earth more than 2000 years ago. For that reason, we have taken many of His parables and teachings and applied them to those of us who love the joy and freedom of the open road.

We hope you tuck this book in your saddlebag (hence the title) and enjoy a story or two as you have a cup of coffee or stop for lunch at a favorite biker dive. In these pages, we would like you to gain a clearer understanding of a God who truly loves you and then ponder the truth of the words you have read as you head out onto the highway. Also, if these words resonate in your heart and soul, then pay it forward and pass this little book along to a friend or a fellow traveler you meet on this road we call "life."

Peace and Ride Safe,

Debbie Edwards

Saints and Sinners

To some who were confident of their own righteousness and looked down on everyone else, Jesus told this parable: "Two men went up to the temple to pray, one a Pharisee and the other a tax collector. The Pharisee stood by himself and prayed: 'God, I thank you that I am not like other people—robbers, evildoers, adulterers—or even like this tax collector. I fast twice a week and give a tenth of all I get.' "But the tax collector stood at a distance. He would not even look up to heaven, but beat his breast and said, 'God, have mercy on me, a sinner.' "I tell you that this man, rather than the other, went home justified before God. For all those who exalt themselves will be humbled, and those who humble themselves will be exalted." (Luke 18:9-14)

I went to college and seminary to become a pastor. For nearly thirty years I worked within the local church, preaching the Gospel and caring for the needs of people. I have taught Bible studies in the prisons, fed the homeless on the streets and on one occasion preached to over eight thousand people in Africa. My last assignment before starting a motorcycle ministry was to plant a church in Southern California where I was the lead pastor for thirteen years; enjoying the love and respect given to most ministers.

One day, after leaving the pastorate and entering full-time motorcycle ministry, I walked into a grocery story to buy a few things. Having ridden there on my bike, I was dressed in the usual sleeveless shirt, chaps, jeans and leather vest. By now, my head was shaved, my beard had grown and I was sporting a few tattoos. My metamorphosis had been gradual so I hadn't given much thought to my appearance, until I noticed for the first time that people were looking at me differently. The realization hit me the hardest when a protective young mother pulled her small child close to her as I walked by. (I turned to see the threat and then realized it was me!) When I was a pastor, children would run to me on Sunday mornings to receive my hugs, but on this day I was the villain; a threat to women and small children! I wanted to shout, "Hey it's me! Pastor Marty!" but that would have only added to their suspicions. It has been said, "You can't judge a book by its cover!" It's what's on the inside that counts.

The Pharisees during Jesus' time were one of three primary religious groups within Judaism; the most influential and vocal of the day. The name "Pharisee" means "separated ones" but they were also known as "chasidim" or "beloved of God." By this time, however, their faith had long since left their hearts and traveled about sixteen inches to their heads; becoming excessively cultic and legalistic about certain parts of the Jewish law, much of which they had created themselves. Many of those who had once been known as "the beloved of God" no longer even recognized Him when they stood in His presence. They were too busy being hyper religious; parading around in elaborate robes, spouting the law and judging other people. Imagine, in this parable, the audacity of a public prayer that says, "God, I thank you that I am not like other people—robbers, evildoers, adulterers—or even like this tax collector." Jesus saw right through him - and he sees into our hearts as well.

Tax collectors were Jews who collected dues from their own people on behalf of the ruling Roman government. Collectors made their living by charging whatever they wanted, over and above what Rome required. The tax collectors were hated and despised by the rest of society; considered to be opportunistic thieves getting rich off of the poor!

We have, therefore, two groups of people represented in this parable and throughout much of the New Testament; the Pharisees (perceived to be "saints") and the tax collectors ("sinners"). While Jesus praised the tax collector for a contrite and repentant heart, He chastised the Pharisee for his pompous religious attitude. The taxman knew he was a sinner, crying out, "God have mercy on me!" while the Pharisee played a role and judged everyone else.

Jesus said to the crowds, "Unless your righteousness exceeds that of the...Pharisees, you will never enter the kingdom of heaven!" (Matthew 5:20) People must have gasped and wondered, "Who then can go to heaven?" But Jesus doesn't look at fancy clothes, pedigrees and churchy talk. He looks at and knows the heart of a man or a woman.

Jesus said that this obvious sinner, because of his genuine repentance, will enter heaven long before the pious windbag. Nothing has changed today. God still looks at our hearts. Doctors, lawyers, preachers and politicians are all the same in the eyes of God. We are all sinners. We all need a Savior and His name is Jesus!

"Know that the LORD has set apart his faithful servant for himself; the LORD hears when I call to him. Tremble and do not sin; when you are on your beds, search your hearts and be silent. Offer the sacrifices of the righteous and trust in the LORD." (Psalm 4:3-5)

Seeds
(The Seeds We Sow - Part I)

...Jesus went out of the house and sat by the lake. Such large crowds gathered around him that he got into a boat and sat in it, while all the people stood on the shore. Then he told them many things in parables, saying: "A farmer went out to sow his seed. As he was scattering the seed, some fell along the path, and the birds came and ate it up. Some fell on rocky places, where it did not have much soil. It sprang up quickly, because the soil was shallow. But when the sun came up, the plants were scorched, and they withered because they had no root. Other seed fell among thorns, which grew up and choked the plants. Still other seed fell on good soil, where it produced a crop—a hundred, sixty or thirty times what was sown." (Matthew 13:1-8)

One of the things I appreciate about the biker community is the opportunity to meet so many colorful characters. "People watching" is my favorite pastime at any motorcycle event. I say that with the utmost love and respect! These are my people! Each rider is so interesting to me; formed and shaped, even chiseled and broken into the person they are today. Unlike the predictable suits that walk up and down Wall Street, bikers are colorful people like cowboys from the old wild west; each one a story waiting to be told.

For every limp and scar there is a tale; an adventure gone bad. With each tattoo there is a town and an interesting person who painstakingly carved their craft into someone's flesh. For every sunburn and wrinkle there is a glorious road trip and destination that came with good friends and nice people they met along the way. Bikers are fascinating people who have made their lives into what they are today.

We have sown our seeds, the good and the bad. We have made our investments of time, money and decisions, contributions to who we are today. The seeds we have planted and watered have now sprouted into irreversible marks on our body, mind and spirit. That's why we need to be thoughtful about the seeds we sow. The Bible even warns us, "Do not be deceived: God cannot be mocked. A man reaps what he sows. Whoever sows to please their flesh, from the flesh will reap destruction; whoever sows to please the Spirit, from the Spirit will reap eternal life." (Galatians 6:7-8)

This parable, however, is not about the seeds that we sow, but about the seed that has been sown within us by God Himself. In the second part of this parable Jesus explains that the seed He speaks of is God's Word and the four soils represent four kinds of hearts. Look carefully in the next chapter and see if you can identify what condition your soil is in. God is speaking to us every day, are we listening? Are we even capable of hearing? Are we distracted? Have we procrastinated and avoided God's message for a time more convenient to our liking? Is it that we don't want to hear from God or have we been swept away by a thousand other lesser attractions that seduce us into spiritual slumber?

"Now then, my children, listen to me; blessed are those who keep my ways. Listen to my instruction and be wise; do not disregard it. Blessed are those who listen to me, watching daily at my doors, waiting at my doorway. For those who find me find life and receive favor from the LORD." (Proverbs 8:32-35)

Seeds
(The Seeds God Sows - Part II)

Jesus said, **"Listen then to what the parable of the sower means: When anyone hears the message about the kingdom and does not understand it, the evil one comes and snatches away what was sown in their heart. This is the seed sown along the path. The seed falling on rocky ground refers to someone who hears the word and at once receives it with joy. But since they have no root, they last only a short time. When trouble or persecution comes because of the word, they quickly fall away. The seed falling among the thorns refers to someone who hears the word, but the worries of this life and the deceitfulness of wealth choke the word, making it unfruitful. But the seed falling on good soil refers to someone who hears the word and understands it. This is the one who produces a crop, yielding a hundred, sixty or thirty times what was sown."** (Matthew 18:23)

In the previous chapter we discussed how we have all become the persons we are today, at least in part, because of the seeds we have sown in the past. Everyone sows seeds; good ones and bad ones, followed by a predictable harvest. This chapter, however, is about our hearts; the soil or ground spoken of in the verses above. In this parable Jesus describes four kinds of soil; hardened paths, rocky ground, thorns and good soil.

A walking path is no place to plant seeds. Paths are hard and dry, having been trampled and compacted by the constant stomping of many feet. Likewise, our hearts can be trampled and hardened by people, disappointments, personal loss and injustice. Time itself can trample our hearts as we continually say "No" to God and resist His voice. The Bible says, "Today, if you hear his voice, do not harden your hearts..." (Hebrews 3:15) Hard hearts do not hear well and often have no feeling.

Rocky ground will receive a good seed, but there is no soil in which the seeds are able to sink their roots. I have spoken with many who have heard and understood the Good News of Christ, but the priorities in their lives have not allowed that news to germinate, take hold and mature. There may be a prayer of repentance followed by a brief season of reading the Bible or visiting a church but before true growth takes place, their faith withers and dies. In other instances seed can fall on otherwise good soil that has been infested with thorns. The seed takes root and begins to sprout, but as it grows the aggressive thorn bushes choke the life out of the young plant.

I have a story for each of these soil types; bikers whom I have met who have (to some degree) accepted the things of God only to have them stolen, wither or be choked away. I could give you their stories, but instead, let me tell you about someone who had an open and ready heart (fertile soil); someone who recognized the need to protect and nurture the gift of God they had received.

It was a typical sunny afternoon in Southern California when Jim, a friend of mine, happened upon an accident on a small country road. A rider and his bike were hopelessly wedged between the asphalt and a Jaguar sedan. The man was crying out in pain as various people pulled and tugged at his body to set him free. Within seconds my friend was in the rider's face, encouraging him, comforting him and praying for him. "Hang in there buddy! Your friends will be here soon!" To which the man answered, "I don't have anyone. It's just me."

In the days that followed Jim visited Michael in the hospital and cared for his most basic needs. Other Christian bikers came around to pray for his recovery and to keep him company. Little by little he learned about God and His Son Jesus Christ. He heard about God's love, mercy and plan of salvation. In time, Michael surrendered his life and heart to Christ and the seed was firmly planted.

Over the next several months, Michael attended church with his new friends and began spending time with them; laughing and realizing that he was no longer alone. The seed was being watered and cared for by many. Several months later, now on crutches, Michael stood in a church meeting and told of his new life in Christ. Fruit was beginning to appear in Michael's heart and a bountiful crop was inevitable.

Where are you in this story? Have you heard that God loves you? Has that Good News landed on a hard path and been trampled under foot? Has the seed fallen among the rocks and not been given the chance to take root? Or has the Good news of Christ been choked out by so many other things in your life? If so, hear the message again: God loves you, forgives you and offers you the gift of peace, joy and eternal life through Jesus Christ. Reading this now is God tossing the seed your way again; perhaps one last time. Jesus said, "Here I am! I stand at the door [of your heart] and knock. If anyone hears my voice and opens the door, I will come in and eat with that person, and they with me." (Revelation 3:20)

"Trust in the LORD with all your heart and lean not on your own understanding; in all your ways submit to him, and he will make your paths straight." (Proverbs 3:5-6)

Riding in the Sand

Jesus said, "Therefore everyone who hears these words of mine and puts them into practice is like a wise man who built his house on the rock. The rain came down, the streams rose, and the winds blew and beat against that house; yet it did not fall, because it had its foundation on the rock. But everyone who hears these words of mine and does not put them into practice is like a foolish man who built his house on sand. The rain came down, the streams rose, and the winds blew and beat against that house, and it fell with a great crash." (Matthew 7:24-27)

A motorcycle is only as stable as the surface it rolls on. Asphalt is good as long as it's not the first rain of the season when the oils of summer still remain. A dirt road isn't a big deal as long as the ground is firm and the ruts are small. The worst conditions I have ever encountered, however, were riding down a mountain one afternoon in late Spring. The little bit of snow that was there in the morning had since melted onto the road and formed into puddles which were now freezing into patches of black ice, fifty to a hundred feet across. One minute I was riding straight and true, then a second later I felt the unmistakable sensation of my rear tire trying to pass me. This went on for about twenty miles before I arrived at the bottom of the hill, where once again, the ground was dry.

Second only to the hazard of ice is sand. Many beautiful paint jobs have been ruined by a small, unexpected patch of sand. It does not matter how good your tires are or how well maintained your machine is, many gifted and experienced riders have been foiled by a little sand on the surface of the road.

Jesus gives us a simple illustration of two builders, one who builds his house on rock and one who builds on sand. The conclusions are predictable. One house came crashing down because its foundations were weak and unreliable. The other house, even when the rains came and the winds blew, stood firm. In fact, Jesus said, "The winds blew and beat against" that house, but it would not fall!

Jesus began this story by giving us two key components for stability. First He said, "Everyone who hears these words of mine…" and then "…puts them into practice." We live in a time when the words of Christ are easily accessible. These words are in Bibles, which in turn are in every church, every bookstore, every library and woven throughout the worldwide internet. But Jesus didn't say "hearing" His words were the key. He said that he who "puts them into practice" will be wise. Knowledge is worthless without application and wisdom is foolishness unless it is heeded.

I don't like riding on soft, unstable and unpredictable surfaces. I don't like the feeling of my tires twitching from side to side as they search for a firm grip. When I ride, I want to feel the rubber tenaciously gripping through a turn! I want to know that my foundation is firm! Isn't it the same for all of life? Who wants to be married to someone who isn't committed? Who wants to go to a job that is guaranteed for one week at a time? Jesus is telling us that we can count on Him if we put into practice what He tells us to do!

Maybe you like earthquakes, but I don't. Having lived in Southern California for most of my life I know what it's like to see the ground roll and tumble like an ocean wave beneath my feet. Life can be like an earthquake with sudden and unexpected shaking and rolling, but many of the unstable situations we encounter are of our own making. If we were to live our lives by the Ten Commandments (Exodus 2) or the Sermon on the Mount (Matthew 5), life in general would be much smoother! Imagine the stability we would enjoy if there was no hatred or murder or adultery. What would it be like if people would not lust and covet and steal? What if everyone just told the truth? What would happen if every human being just treated others in the same way that they would want to be treated? These are the foundation blocks that Christ is offering us. So that even when the rains come down, the winds blow and beat against our lives, we can stand and not fall! Imagine that!

Jesus said, "In this world you WILL have trouble (the winds will blow and the rains will fall). But take heart! I have overcome the world." (John 16:33) In order to regain your footing and maintain your traction, trust in Christ!

"Teach me to do your will, for you are my God; may your good Spirit lead me on level ground." (Psalm 143:10)

The Pearl

Jesus said, **"The kingdom of heaven is like a merchant looking for fine pearls. When he found one of great value, he went away and sold everything he had and bought it."** (Matthew 13:45-46)

Most self-respecting bikers would claim they don't have much need or interest in pearls. Truth is, everybody is interested in pearls! Not necessarily those shiny little gems that grow inside of an oyster shell, but the kind that we lose sleep over at night and dream about throughout the day.

Your "pearl" might be the new touring edition that you saw sitting in the front window of the dealership, or maybe something less tangible like that trip you have always wanted to take across the country. A "pearl" is that one thing you are willing to scrimp and save for and maybe work a lot of overtime to purchase. A "pearl" is something that you just have to have and you will never rest until you get it. Once you have it, you will never let it go!

I realize that those reading this book probably ride all kinds of motorcycles, metric and American. As for me, when I first got "the itch" to buy a bike I had one "pearl" in mind: a Harley-Davidson! After looking at all of the various models, my wife asked a ridiculous question: "What if we can't afford a Harley?" There was no second choice! There was no "plan B!" I was like a spoiled brat in the toy store! I honestly wanted a Harley-Davidson or nothing at all! I wanted to take part in the history and the Americana that comes with riding

21

a Harley! I know that won't make sense to those of you who ride a beautiful Honda or BMW, but that's just where my head was at the time. THAT was my pearl and short of robbing a bank, I was going to get one!

The pearl that Jesus is speaking of here is the kingdom of heaven! Like most treasures, the kingdom of heaven is hidden simply because people are not looking for it. We have settled for the lesser prizes of life. The temporary satisfaction of trinkets can so easily replace the grand treasures of the kingdom! Jesus says, once someone discovers that GREAT pearl, no price will be too great to pay to insure that we get it – and keep it!

My friend Bill was a veteran of World War II and had been captured by the Japanese in the South Pacific. When they found out that he was a Christian they beat him and persecuted him for his faith. As the war was coming to an end, the Japanese began their evacuations. Bill was given one last opportunity to denounce his faith. When he refused, an officer put a saber in his mouth and thrust it up through his head. He was left for dead but was later found alive by American soldiers.

Bill had found a great treasure! His treasure was his faith in Jesus Christ and NOTHING was more valuable to him. All he had to do was pretend to deny his faith and perhaps he would have been spared this torture and near death. But he knew what he had, a great pearl, and he wasn't about to give it up! During his latter years, when I knew Bill, he suffered from severe headaches and extremely poor eyesight, a condition caused by his wounds. Nevertheless, Bill always spoke of the incident with a smile on his face, happy to trade his eyesight for this great treasure of Christ.

What would you die for? What would you give everything you have to attain and keep? That is your pearl! The question is, "How long will your treasure last?" Jesus asked, "What good will it be for someone to gain the whole world, yet forfeit their soul?" (Matthew 16:26) We can spend our lives gathering up all the tinsel that this world has to offer, or we can make one grand sacrifice for that which is truly priceless.

"Surely everyone goes around like a mere phantom; in vain they rush about, heaping up wealth without knowing whose it will finally be. But now, Lord, what do I look for? My hope is in you." (Psalm 39:6-7)

Sticker Shock

Large crowds were traveling with Jesus, and turning to them he said: "If anyone comes to me and does not hate father and mother, wife and children, brothers and sisters—yes, even their own life—such a person cannot be my disciple. And whoever does not carry their cross and follow me cannot be my disciple.

Suppose one of you wants to build a tower. Won't you first sit down and estimate the cost to see if you have enough money to complete it? For if you lay the foundation and are not able to finish it, everyone who sees it will ridicule you, saying, 'This person began to build and wasn't able to finish.'

Or suppose a king is about to go to war against another king. Won't he first sit down and consider whether he is able with ten thousand men to oppose the one coming against him with twenty thousand? If he is not able, he will send a delegation while the other is still a long way off and will ask for terms of peace. In the same way, those of you who do not give up everything you have cannot be my disciples..." (Luke 14:25-33)

It's an easy thing to buy something. Paying for it is another matter. Twice now I have customized my bikes and both times have under estimated what it was going to cost for the paint, the parts and the labor. I had a vision in my head of the colors, the fabrications and the chrome! (Oh, how we love the shiny stuff!) But in the end I was stretched to pay the builders, because I had not first counted the cost. My bank account suffered and my wife was something less than pleased.

Today, we often talk about people who are "born again" or "believers." While both terms are legitimate and have merit, in and of themselves they fall short of describing what it really means to be a disciple of Jesus Christ. The Bible says, "You believe that there is one God. Good! Even the demons believe that – and shudder!" (James 2:19) In other words, "You believe there is a god? So what? A lot of people believe. The devil himself believes!" There's more, however, to being a Christian than just passive acceptance. There is a cost analysis that must first be considered.

Jesus makes some pretty radical statements concerning our notion to follow Him. He gives the analogy of a builder counting the cost of a project and a military leader assessing his chances of victory. But most shocking is His statement, "If anyone comes to me and does not hate" his family, even his own life, he is not worthy to be called a Christian. In other words, we must love God far more than even our own family and dearest friends.

"Sticker shock" is a term used to describe what happens to a buyer looking to purchase an expensive item. You see this year's model sitting on the showroom floor. It is beautiful! It's your color! It fits perfectly as you sit on it, reach for the pedals and drag your fingers across the new paint. Then, without even thinking, you reach for the big yellow price tag swinging from the handlebars and it hits you in the face like a hard passed basketball! Your eyes begin to water and your nose starts to run. You're experiencing STICKER SHOCK! As your heart beats faster, your hands begin to sweat, and you have a decision to make; an assessment: "Can I afford this bike? Do I WANT to afford this bike?" A little voice inside your head says, "You had better take some time and think about this one!"

That's all Jesus is saying, "Take some time and really think about this!" If you're going to follow Jesus, He must be more important to you than anything or anyone. That's not to say that we "pay" for His love or our salvation, but that following Him can be second to no person, no dream, no career, nothing! We become servants of the Most High God.

Throughout scripture, Jesus is referred to as "Lord." The lord is the master of the house; the one who is in leadership and control. The statement, "No, Lord" is actually an oxymoron. When we say "no" to God, He in essence ceases to be the key influence in our lives. Many people call themselves Christians (i.e. followers or disciples of Christ) but their lives tell another story. Obeying God is replaced with, "But I always thought…" and "It just seems right…" We justify what we want with lame excuses such as, "If it feels this good it just can't be wrong!" or "Surely God would want for me to be happy!" (God is not nearly as concerned with our happiness as He is with our obedience.)

Do you truly want to follow Christ? Are you ready to lay your life down for Him? You had better count the cost first! It isn't that much - just everything you have; all of your heart, all your mind, all of your body and all of your soul.

"Come, let us bow down in worship, let us kneel before the LORD our Maker; for he is our God and we are the people of his pasture, the flock under his care." (Psalm 95:6-7)

Rebels
The Prodigal's Return (Part I)

Jesus told a story **"There was a man who had two sons. The younger one said to his father, 'Father, give me my share of the estate.' So he divided his property between them. Not long after that, the younger son got together all he had, set off for a distant country and there squandered his wealth in wild living. After he had spent everything, there was a severe famine in that whole country, and he began to be in need. So he went and hired himself out to a citizen of that country, who sent him to his fields to feed pigs. He longed to fill his stomach with the pods that the pigs were eating, but no one gave him anything.**

When he came to his senses, he said, 'How many of my father's hired servants have food to spare, and here I am starving to death! I will set out and go back to my father and say to him: Father, I have sinned against heaven and against you. I am no longer worthy to be called your son; make me like one of your hired servants.' So he got up and went to his father..." (Luke 15:11-20)

You say, "rebel" like it's a bad thing! Yeah, I'm a rebel and if you ride a bike you're probably a rebel too. We rebel against all of the statistics that say motorcycles are too dangerous and all of the Volvo owners who say we need to grow up. We rebel by preferring jeans and tee shirts over suits and ties and we eat barbecue instead of salad. Some bikers grow their hair long while others shave their heads altogether. We're spotted with tattoos and piercings, leather and chrome studs and have a tendency to unintentionally "part the waters" as we move through a neighborhood shopping mall.

I have a helmet sticker that reads, "Before one can be old and wise, he must first be young and foolish." Every young person has a little rebel in them. If they didn't, they would never leave home. Jesus doesn't tell us why the younger brother in this parable wanted to leave home, but his story isn't that different from so many of ours. Sometimes there is an argument followed by the slamming of doors and sometimes children just move away. Some rebels make a scene while others pretend to be compliant while burning on the inside.

Whatever our young man did wrong, he also did a few things right. First, he eventually came to his senses when so many never do. Second, he had the courage to say, "Enough is enough!" He owned his mistakes, blamed no one but himself and had the humility to go home. Furthermore, he doesn't seem to have had any sense of entitlement or expectation and he's not expecting to return to his family as a son, but as a servant. He's ready to take his medicine.

If you haven't figured it out yet, Jesus is talking to so many of us who have run away and done our own thing. Some of us have done well in our rebellion and made a lot of money while others have dined at the table of pigs. But success is not defined so much by money and things as it is by peace and joy. What Jesus is trying to communicate is that failing is human and it's ok to come home. Jesus says, "Come to me, all of you who are weary and burdened, and I will give you rest." (Matthew 3:14)

Some things need to be rebelled against while others need to be embraced and strictly obeyed. I would suggest that you not rebel against things like gravity, electricity and God. You certainly have the freedom to step off of a twenty story building or stick a fork in a light socket – let me know how that works out for you. But while many continue to rebel against God, God doesn't shrink or fade. He stands firm and consistent. He is good and He is right. He is waiting for rebels to come home.

"If you, LORD, kept a record of sins...who could stand? But with you there is forgiveness, so that we can, with reverence, serve you." (Psalm 130:3-4)

Rebels
A Father's Welcome (Part II)

Jesus continued His story… **"But while he was still a long way off, his father saw him and was filled with compassion for him; he ran to his son, threw his arms around him and kissed him. The son said to him, 'Father, I have sinned against heaven and against you. I am no longer worthy to be called your son.' But the father said to his servants, 'Quick! Bring the best robe and put it on him. Put a ring on his finger and sandals on his feet. Bring the fattened calf and kill it. Let's have a feast and celebrate. For this son of mine was dead and is alive again; he was lost and is found.' So they began to celebrate."** (Luke 15:20-24)

A sixteen-year-old boy was driving too fast and didn't see the stop sign in time. Evidently he didn't see the bikers who were coming through the intersection either. Both of these riders were my friends, one of which was struck hard on the left side of his scooter, crushing his leg and foot. In all directions cars came to a screeching halt and soon the police and paramedics were on the scene. What could have easily killed my friend, instead resulted in months of therapy, a limp that would never go away and a motorcycle that had to be rebuilt courtesy of an insurance policy.

As the fire engines and paramedics pulled away, there was still a very scared and confused sixteen-year-old young man sitting in his pick-up truck. His dad sat next to him, comforting and lecturing him at the same time. The boy's anxiety wasn't helped when the other biker approached the two in the truck. My friend was well over six feet tall, three hundred pounds and had long black hair and a full beard to match. Expecting the worst, perhaps even a physical altercation, the two in the truck were stunned when my friend asked, "How are you guys doing? Everyone alright?" He went on to console the young man, assuring him that the injured rider would recover and that everything would work out. Then he did the unthinkable. The biker asked if he could pray for the father and son. When he was done praying he winked at the boy, shook the father's hand and rode away to join his buddy who was on his way to the emergency room.

Certainly there was some kind of a settlement between insurance companies, but between driver and rider there was nothing more than consolation and forgiveness. There were no lectures, no threats and certainly no ridiculous lawsuits. Lessons were learned and people were forgiven – in the name of Christ.

The young prodigal in Luke chapter 15 had suffered a major crash! He was tired, hungry and dragging himself home to what would no doubt be an even worse experience. All he was hoping for was some food, a safe place to sleep and perhaps a job. Understand, that in the Jewish way of thinking, this boy was dead to his family. He had nothing to come home to according to traditional laws and customs. He had spent his inheritance and there was nothing left. He was a disgrace and a failure and he had no one to blame but himself. The story reads, however, that while he was still a long way off, his father saw him and ran to him.

The only way the father could have seen his son from a great distance is that he must have been looking for him – anticipating and hoping for his return. And when the son began his confession it seems that the father just ignored him, shouting orders for clean clothes, new shoes, preparations for a giant barbeque – and the family ring. In this society only slaves went barefoot and only family members wore the family ring. The father had no interest in lecturing his son or having him grovel his way back. It simply reads, "…while he was still a long way off, his father saw him and was filled with compassion for him; he ran to his son, threw his arms around him and kissed him."

The Bible tells us, "God demonstrates his own love for us in this: While we were still sinners, Christ died for us." (Romans 5:8) Nobody had to tell the boy in the pick-up that he had made a bad mistake, and nobody needs to tell you and me that we are sinners – we get it! Likewise, the younger brother who took his inheritance and ran away had also made some very bad mistakes. But there is a time for chastisement and there is a time for forgiveness and that is why the father in this story is as much of a rebel as his son.

You see, this story is typically referred to as "the prodigal son." We might think of the word prodigal as meaning "runaway" but what it really means is "to spend freely." And while yes, the son spent his inheritance in a free and reckless manner, his father spent his forgiveness and mercy freely as well; recklessly ignoring what people would say. The father risked much to welcome his son home. He wagered his reputation with the community and his relationship with his older son who had stayed home, obedient and silent.

Our Father in heaven "broke the bank" when He sent His son Jesus to earth, to die on a cross as a payment for our sins. It wasn't fair, but it was merciful! Just like this earthly father, our Father in Heaven wants for His children to come home. He knows we are sinners and we know it too. All is forgiven. Just come home.

"Have mercy on me, O God, according to your unfailing love; according to your great compassion blot out my transgressions. Wash away all my iniquity and cleanse me from my sin." (Psalm 51:1-2)

Rebels
Born to Be Mild (Part III)

Jesus continued His story… **"Meanwhile, the older son was in the field. When he came near the house, he heard music and dancing. So he called one of the servants and asked him what was going on. 'Your brother has come,' he replied, 'and your father has killed the fattened calf because he has him back safe and sound.' The older brother became angry and refused to go in. So his father went out and pleaded with him. But he answered his father, 'Look! All these years I've been slaving for you and never disobeyed your orders. Yet you never gave me even a young goat so I could celebrate with my friends. But when this son of yours who has squandered your property with prostitutes comes home, you kill the fattened calf for him!' 'My son,' the father said, 'you are always with me, and everything I have is yours. But we had to celebrate and be glad, because this brother of yours was dead and is alive again; he was lost and is found.'"** (Luke 15:25-32)

Maybe you were a real wild child, born to be wild and have been raising hell ever since kindergarten. You were the first one to take a dare, the first one to get hurt and the first one to end up in the principal's office. You were also the last one to get a job, the last one to leave the bar and the last one to admit that you were scared or needed help. So you're a rebel? Great! But even rebels get tired and hungry and eventually need to come to their senses.

Perhaps you're one of those rebels who made it home and, in spite of all the wild oats sown, you discovered a second chance, a new life and mercy at the end of your rope. Maybe you're one of the lucky ones who had a family waiting for you, more interested in forgiveness and restoration than blame and condemnation. Second chances are rare and are not to be wasted.

Or maybe you're the one who stayed home, went to class every day, passed all of your tests and did homework on the weekends while others were out having a good time. It's tough being the guy who's first at the office in the morning and the last to leave at night. You're the older brother, old faithful, the one that everyone can count on – and you're resenting every second of it, ready to explode! You did the right things for all of the wrong reasons and now you're bitter and angry and feel as if life has passed you by.

To make matters worse, your little brother ran away, had is fun, spent your dad's hard earned money and now he comes trotting back home only to be treated like a rock star! Words like "grace" and "mercy" and "forgiveness" applied to the irresponsible losers of this world make you sick! How about a little old fashioned justice? "Tell my little brother to pound sand, hit the road, get lost." These days he might just tell his little brother to "Go to hell!" But if he does, he rebels against God's plan for all little brothers.

Some rebels wear leather. Some wear sensible blue suits. It all depends on what they are rebelling against. I've always appreciated the honesty that I have found in the biker community. People say what they think and let the chips fall where they may. It's the "respectable" members of society who are polite, hold their peace and talk about you behind your back that concern me! It's the quiet rebels that wave their flags of responsibility but burn on the inside for some creative expression of self that frighten me! One day, they will suddenly explode! "All these years I've been slaving for you and never disobeyed your orders. Yet you never gave me even a young goat so I could celebrate with my friends. But when this son of yours who has squandered your property with prostitutes comes home, you kill the fattened calf for him!" In a moment when he could no longer keep his emotions in check the older son erupts against the notions of "grace" and "mercy" and "forgiveness."

The inability to forgive is a horrible thing. Unforgiveness is like a pebble in your shoe, producing a raw blister that only gets worse with time. Others have described unforgiveness as a cancer that if left unattended will eat its host alive. The urgency to forgive others is not so much their need for our approval, but our need to be rid of the deadly toxins that will certainly destroy us.

The older brother assumes that his younger sibling had just gotten away with murder! But please note that the father never said to his youngest son, "Oh, that's alright! You meant well." We don't know what consequences awaited the young prodigal, but we certainly don't have much evidence that his inheritance was restored. The father simply forgave him and celebrated his return.

We don't know if the older brother ever got over his anger towards his father and younger sibling, the story doesn't say. But Jesus' parable is easily understood and should be embraced by all rebels: God the Father forgives sinners and welcomes them home when they are ready to return. Some will not easily accept such amazing grace, misunderstanding it for injustice. What the older son fails to see, however, are the sins of his younger brother hanging on the cross with Jesus, right alongside of his own and yours and mine.

"Blessed is the one whose transgressions are forgiven, whose sins are covered. Blessed is the one whose sin the LORD does not count against them and in whose spirit is no deceit." (Psalm 32:1-2)

Chrome Won't Get You Home

Jesus said, **"The ground of a certain rich man yielded an abundant harvest. He thought to himself, 'What shall I do? I have no place to store my crops.' Then he said, 'This is what I'll do. I will tear down my barns and build bigger ones, and there I will store my surplus grain. And I'll say to myself, 'You have plenty of grain laid up for many years. Take life easy; eat, drink and be merry.'" But God said to him, 'You fool! This very night your life will be demanded from you. Then who will get what you have prepared for yourself?' This is how it will be with whoever stores up things for themselves but is not rich toward God."** (Luke 12:16-21)

Bikers say, "Chrome won't get you home!" meaning, "all of that glitz and shine is fine, but it's what's inside the bike that counts." Trailer queens (bikes that travel from place to place in or on a trailer) are said to be "all show and no go." Furthermore, when a motorcycle is resold, most will find very little resale value in that custom paint job and excessive chrome. In the end, a Fat Boy is a Fat Boy no matter how you have customized it.

Jesus tells the story of a man who has everything. Problem is, none of us ever really have "everything" and so those looking for security or prestige find it necessary to just keep acquiring more and more stuff. I'm guilty! I remember thinking that if I could actually afford a new Harley-Davidson I would have "arrived." But after buying my first bike, it was only a few hundred miles later that I began to crave a custom paint job and a truckload of chrome! Contentment escaped me.

In this story, a farmer has an abundant crop, so much so that he has no place to put his surplus. (In America we pay for storage units in which to keep the things we will never consume or use.) So the farmer sets out to build another barn and thinks that then he will be ready for the "good life." Later that night, however, he dies and Jesus calls him a "fool." In death, prestige, power and possessions mean nothing. "You can't take it with you" is the truth! Only one thing matters in death: God and your relationship with Him. "He who dies with the most toys wins…nothing!"

This farmer makes two common mistakes. First, he assumes that God's many blessings are just for him. Eight times in this short story the farmer uses the words, "I" and "my" and "myself." Later in this passage Jesus will say, "From everyone who has been given much, much will be required; and from the one who has been entrusted with much, much more will be asked." That is to say, wealth is not only a privilege, but a responsibility. We are merely stewards of the wealth that God has entrusted to us. We are responsible for how we use it.

Secondly, this farmer seems to be a self made man. He has worked hard all of his life and saved and is now ready for retirement. His answer to happiness and security is to stockpile surplus wealth for his old age. I'm thinking about the new rider who is so excited about his new bike – he forgets to take a motorcycle safety course. This farmer "looked" prepared but God says he is a fool for missing the most important things in life. Everybody dies. Everybody! God does not condemn the farmer's wealth but his complete lack of planning for the eternal things.

Most Americans believe in God. A 2008 poll by the Washington Post determined that 92% of us believe in God or a universal spirit.

The poll also concluded that more than half pray every day. This begs the question, "If we know we're going to die…and most of us believe that something or someone is waiting on the other side of death, why then are we not making preparations for life after death?" We prepare for life and we prepare for old age – but why not death? It's certainly coming for each of us. Are you so sure you know what's on the other side? You have prepared well for the here and now, but what about tomorrow?

Jesus said, "Do not store up for yourselves treasures on earth, where moths and vermin destroy, and where thieves break in and steal. For where your treasure is, there your heart will be also." (Matthew 6:19-21) In our lifetime we will spend hundreds of thousands (for some millions) of dollars on things that will rust and decay. I say "spend" because such things are not an investment. The Bible describes life as a "vapor"- like steam escaping from a kettle. It comes and goes so quickly, as anyone over fifty can attest.

Is your life "all show" and not prepared "to go?" Are you investing only for the "here and now" but neglecting what is to come? What if this night your soul becomes required of you? Are you ready to ride?

"Better is one day in your courts than a thousand elsewhere; I would rather be a doorkeeper in the house of my God than dwell in the tents of the wicked. For the LORD God is a sun and shield; the LORD bestows favor and honor; no good thing does he withhold from those whose walk is blameless." (Psalm 84:10-11)

No One Left Behind

Jesus said, **"Suppose one of you has a hundred sheep and loses one of them. Doesn't he leave the ninety-nine in the open country and go after the lost sheep until he finds it? And when he finds it, he joyfully puts it on his shoulders and goes home. Then he calls his friends and neighbors together and says, 'Rejoice with me; I have found my lost sheep.' I tell you that in the same way there will be more rejoicing in heaven over one sinner who repents than over ninety-nine righteous persons who do not need to repent."** (Luke 14:4-7)

The wife and I were on our way back from Sturgis Bike Week, admiring the corn fields of Nebraska, when suddenly the back of the bike felt sloppy and sluggish. Fifty miles from anywhere we had a flat tire, a cell phone without a signal and no one riding with us to go get help. After waiting for more than an hour, we began to pray and ask God to rescue us. One of us suggested, "Try the phone again!" - even though we had had no service since the day before. With little more than a whisper of faith we dialed one more time and held our breath. IT WORKED! It was an hour before the tow truck arrived, but it's hard to describe how good it felt to hear another human being on the other end of our line, meaning that we would NOT be spending the night on the side of a highway somewhere in Nebraska.

We were alone on that particular trip, but had we been riding with friends someone would certainly have stayed with us while someone else went for help. The biker code demands that no one is left behind - and only a complete jerk would pass a fellow rider stranded on the side of the road! Real bikers just don't do that to one another!

Jesus must feel the same way since He spoke in this parable of the value of one. It could have been argued, "Hey, why should we have to sit out here in the sun just because your bike broke down?" Some may also argue, "I've lost one sheep, but I've got ninety-nine more. What's the big deal?" Jesus, however, insists that any good shepherd would leave the ninety-nine for the one that was missing. In fact, He stresses that the shepherd leaves the ninety-nine in "open country," signifying the risk involved. Wolves and other wild beasts are in the open country as are thieves, but for God, EVERYONE is important. He will not stop looking until they are found!

I'm not sure who said it first, but the saying goes, "If I were the only human on the entire planet, God would have sent Jesus to die for my sins." Do you believe that? You need to! You are THAT important to God. You are as important to Him as Billy Graham or Mother Teresa. All of the sheep are loved the same; the fat ones, the ugly ones and even the dumb ones! You are loved and worthy of being found!

Jesus didn't tell us this parable to stress the importance of taking care of our livestock. We're talking about people here, men and women made in God's image! (Genesis 1:26) In this chapter, Jesus tells three consecutive parables about something or someone precious that was lost; a lost sheep, a lost coin and His finale, a lost son. In each case, when that which is lost is found, a full-blown party breaks out! Friends, neighbors and even angels come together and rejoice!

Jesus will never leave you sitting on the side of the road alone. Even if He needs to tell everyone else to wait, He'll come back for you! He promised us, "I will not leave you as orphans..." (John 14:18),

"Never will I leave you; never will I forsake you." (Hebrews 13:5) Jesus understands the code; no one left behind.

"Let me live that I may praise you, and may your laws sustain me. I have strayed like a lost sheep. Seek your servant, for I have not forgotten your commands." (Psalm 119:175-176)

U-Turns Allowed

Jesus asked, **"What do you think? There was a man who had two sons. He went to the first and said, 'Son, go and work today in the vineyard.' 'I will not,' he answered, but later he changed his mind and went. Then the father went to the other son and said the same thing. He answered, 'I will, sir,' but he did not go. Which of the two did what his father wanted?"** (Matthew 21:28-32)

One of my favorite biker quotes is, "It's the journey, not the destination." OK - I get it! It's all of the things that happen along the way that make for a good trip – not simply arriving in a timely fashion. My first trip to Sturgis, SD was in 2003 and it was the best adventure of my life up until that point, but it had very little to do with the town of Sturgis. What made that trip so memorable was the ride, the wind, the scenery, all of the places we stopped at along the way and all of the interesting people we met. It was a thirty-two hundred mile roundtrip adventure that my wife and I will never forget!

On the other hand, the destination is important as well – right? Without a destination I might still be "on my way" to Sturgis! Furthermore, as much as I enjoyed that trip in 2003, a journey without accurate directions and an eventual destination is just being lost! And if you're lost (gentlemen!) you might need to admit that you are lost and stop to ask for directions. Only then can you make the necessary course changes.

A man had two sons. Both left their father for a short time and both changed directions mid-journey. They were both asked to go into the field and work. One said, "No" but ended up changing directions and obeyed his father. The other sounded good as he acquiesced, but never really meant to follow through in obedience. Jesus asked the question, "Which of the two sons were obedient?" The answer is clear: the one who made a u-turn.

I have a riding buddy who has the road name, "U-Turn." I've never asked him the details about his life before becoming a Christian, but I know that it was one of rebellion and disobedience towards God and anything wholesome. Today, he is emphatic that "God allows for u-turns in life."

Some of us start out life like the first son; full of steam, grand ideas and absolute independence. We do a burn out leaving the driveway determined to discover life on our own terms – as fast as we can. We say "no" to nothing! We live the "good life" and end up with the scars to show it. At some point we come to our senses and return to what we know is right.

Others of us identify with the second son. We started off all right; the favorite son of the parents who did well in school, voted "Most Likely to Succeed" and joined the family business. Everybody was so proud of us! Then one day, we just couldn't take it anymore! "KA-BOOM!" We exploded and began to write checks that our bodies could not cover. (Sometimes we call this a mid-life crisis.) We suddenly found ourselves doing all of the things we really wanted to do when we were younger.

Jesus is directing this parable to the second brothers. They are religious men who say "yes" and play the part of the obedient child, but inside they are as angry and rebellious as they can be. In their self-righteous rage they lash out at the masses who are now coming to Christ in repentance. "How dare that prostitute…that tax collector… that sinner come to God now… after all they have done." They "dare" to do so because they have been invited. They have been forgiven.

That's what Jesus does, He allows u-turns. It is never too late to stop and make things right. God is waiting. Turn around and see.

"Out of the depths I cry to you, LORD; Lord, hear my voice. Let your ears be attentive to my cry for mercy. If you, LORD, kept a record of sins, Lord, who could stand? But with you there is forgiveness, so that we can, with reverence, serve you" (Psalm 130: 1-4)

Life Is For Living

Jesus said to His followers, **"You are the salt of the earth; but if the salt loses its flavor, how shall it be seasoned? It is then good for nothing but to be thrown out and trampled underfoot by men. You are the light of the world. A city that is set on a hill cannot be hidden. Nor do they light a lamp and put it under a basket, but on a lamp stand, and it gives light to all who are in the house. Let your light so shine before men, that they may see your good works and glorify your Father in heaven."** (Matthew 5:13-16)

Tony had little interest in knowing or finding out anything about God. What he already knew suited him just fine. Brought up in a strict and often punitive religious home, legalism was the order of the day. Church was a bore and so were the people who went there!

Rules were enforced with rigidity and the people in the small town church where he grew up were kind but didn't seem to have a lot of joy or fun for that matter. Sunday was more than a day of rest, it was a day of forced boredom; sheer torture for an energetic little boy. The adults in his life said, "God wanted it that way."

When Tony moved out on his own and got to make his own decisions church was the last place he wanted to be on Sunday. He bought a motorcycle and finally began to enjoy "the day of rest." He experienced a freedom and exhilaration he had only dreamed of when he was younger. Riding became his new religion and his riding buddies his new "church group." But even though Tony celebrated the sun, the wind and nature at its best, he had no concept of who had made it and no idea to whom credit was due.

Tony's childhood experiences effectively erected roadblocks in his life preventing him from experiencing a real and meaningful understanding and relationship with God. The Christians in Tony's world had seriously wounded his spirit with their absence of spice and were certainly no light that would have inspired or encouraged an all American boy. What a shame.

Jesus used parables, common things like salt and light, to convey truth to His listeners. For instance, everyone needs light to get around in the darkness. Have you ever been driving out in the country at night and just for the fun of it turned your headlamps off - even if just for a second? What a shock! In the darkness you are helpless and vulnerable. You can't see what to avoid and you can't tell what might be coming at you. When the light comes, however, even shadows are illuminated and all is made clear. What was hazy now becomes bright. God's word is described to us as light which is able to illuminate spiritual darkness and replace it with peace and understanding.

Jesus may have spoken to Tony about salt as well: Salt in the ancient world was valuable and even necessary for life. It gave food flavor and preserved meat from spoiling. A relationship with God not only flavors our lives, it preserves us as we trust in Him who has our best interest at heart. When you discover that God REALLY loves you and cares about you, there can be a deep sense of satisfaction and security.

These things had never been modeled for Tony. God and church didn't illuminate anything for the boy. They were just icons of "don't do this" and "don't do that!" As for spice and flavor, religion has none. It's a personal and intimate relationship with God in the person of Jesus Christ that is truly exciting! You don't need to sell your motorcycle, stop listening to good music or even quit bungee jumping! Just include God in your life; the spice of life! In fact, Jesus said, "I have come that [you] may have life, and have it to the full!" (John 10:10)

Don't shut God out because of a preconceived notion of "religion." We apologize for our Christian brothers and sisters who may have been dim and bland in their presentation of the Gospel. We're sure they meant well, but God is good and exciting! Life is at its best when Jesus is at the center.

"The law of the LORD is perfect, refreshing the soul. The statutes of the LORD are trustworthy, making wise the simple. The precepts of the LORD are right, giving joy to the heart. The commands of the LORD are radiant, giving light to the eyes. The fear of the LORD is pure, enduring forever. The decrees of the LORD are firm, and all of them are righteous. They are more precious than gold, than much pure gold; they are sweeter than honey, than honey from the honeycomb." (Psalm 19:7-10)

You Gotta Ask

Jesus said, **"Suppose you have a friend, and you go to him at midnight and say, 'Friend, lend me three loaves of bread; a friend of mine on a journey has come to me, and I have no food to offer him.' And suppose the one inside answers, 'Don't bother me. The door is already locked, and my children and I are in bed. I can't get up and give you anything.' I tell you, even though he will not get up and give you the bread because of friendship, yet because of your shameless audacity he will surely get up and give you as much as you need. So I say to you: Ask and it will be given to you; seek and you will find; knock and the door will be opened to you. For everyone who asks receives; the one who seeks finds; and to the one who knocks, the door will be opened."** (Luke 11:5-10)

We used to ride an older Evo; our first Harley. She was a beautiful bike but as the miles began to pile up she developed a few quirky problems. One of her favorite ways to make a ride interesting was to suddenly and without notice surprise us with a dead battery. Marty changed the battery and had all the wiring checked, but nothing we did seemed to fix the problem.

One summer we rode the bike through Yellowstone National Park. We pulled off at all the scenic turnouts, checking out the natural beauty and wildlife. We had stopped to photograph a flock of Canadian geese and when we got back on the bike.....you guessed it - "Eloise" decided to take an extended rest break.... we had NO POWER!

My husband groaned and tromped out to the roadside to try to get someone with jumper cables to stop and help us out. (Do you know how many tourists there are in Yellowstone...in rental cars... who don't speak English?) After about fifteen minutes of motorists not bothering to stop for him, I thought I might need to come to his rescue! It occurred to me that Marty looked way too scary for anyone to risk getting involved with this guy. I wouldn't have stopped for him if I was a tourist! With his bald head, dark glasses and biker cut, people just drove right by ignoring him as he tried to wave them down. But when I went out to the road and sent him back to the bike, a nice family stopped within five minutes, complete with a functional set of jumper cables. The point is, we had to ask and we had to keep on asking until someone stopped. We were stuck! We could not fix this one by ourselves.

Jesus uses this parable to show His disciples what we can expect from a God who has what we need but does not owe us anything. In Jesus' time, when travelers arrived at your home, they were always served a meal. To fail to do so would have been considered rude and inhospitable. So when this man's guests arrived in the middle of the night and he realized he had no bread to offer them, he begged his neighbor to help him out. Sure, it must have been embarrassing to stand out there in the night banging on his friend's door, but what else was he going to do? He was in a bind! He had to ask!

In contrast to this neighbor who was tucked in for the night and not interested in helping his friend, Jesus paints a picture of a loving and willing God who is eager and waiting for us to come to Him. Our God is generous, compassionate and ready to give us what we need, but we need to ask. The Bible tells us, "You do not have because you do not ask God." (James 4:2)

How about you? Are you willing to humble yourself and ask - even if it means walking out of the house in your pajamas at midnight? Or are you the self sufficient type who thinks they have it all under control? Maybe you think you have enough money to cover whatever comes your way or enough friends or enough of whatever. Don't bet on it! You have a heavenly Father willing and waiting with open arms if you put aside your pride and "can do" attitude and become willing to ask Him to satisfy your needs and then trust that He will answer.

"The LORD is a refuge for the oppressed, a stronghold in times of trouble. Those who know your name trust in you, for you, LORD, have never forsaken those who seek you." (Psalm 9:9-10)

Selling Out

Jesus said, **"The kingdom of heaven is like treasure hidden in a field. When a man found it, he hid it again, and then in his joy went and sold all he had and bought that field."** (Matthew 13:44)

Some people buy a motorcycle and decorate their garage with it while others ctually like to ride! Many owners discover a whole new lifestyle with their bike which includes riding every spare afternoon and weekend. They discover a whole new group of friends, new places to go and new things to do! When someone in their group sells their bike to buy a boat or an SUV everyone persecutes them mercilessly for "selling out!" (I've witnessed it personally and it's not pretty!)

Sometimes, however, "selling out" can be a good thing. In a sense, you sold out when you got married. You had to sell your Corvette for a bigger car and leave behind your customized bachelor pad and waterbed for a three bedroom mortgage and a swing set. Twenty years later, however, you admit that it was worth it.

Imagine one afternoon walking across an abandoned piece of property not far from your house. Kicking the can in front of you, you discover just the very small corner of a partially buried steamer trunk. Years of rain and wind have eroded the topsoil exposing just the smallest corner of the rusty old box. At first you're just a little bit curious so you poke around it with a stick. As your interest grows so does your breathing! "This is really cool! This could be something great!" Then before long you realize that this box is bigger than you thought and heavier than you will ever be able to carry home by yourself. Besides, "Whose land is this? Did anyone see me?"

Jabbing the prize with the stick a soft portion of the trunk is breeched and the contents are revealed. IT'S MONEY! There are what seems to be hundreds of gold coins and bundles of one hundred dollar bills, each one staring back at you as if to say, "Come and get me!"

What would you do to be able to take that box home with you? You might need to buy the property. You might need to sell your car, your boat or even your...Harley! Would you miss work the next day to explore the possibilities? Would you quit your job altogether? What would you do for a treasure like that?

In this parable, Jesus suggests if you want a treasure badly enough, you will do anything and give EVERYTHING to get it! Unfortunately, that's what some people are thinking just before they rob a bank or steal a car. But in the case of heavenly treasure, nobody needs to steal because anybody can afford it. All this treasure costs is "all that you have."

You protest, "That's too much! I don't want to give up my life and my way of doing things." To you Jesus would say, "Whoever wants to be my disciple must deny themselves and take up their cross and follow me. For whoever wants to save their life will lose it, but whoever loses their life for me and for the gospel will save it. What good is it for someone to gain the whole world, yet forfeit their soul? Or what can anyone give in exchange for their soul?" (Mark 8:34-37)

What could be more precious than eternal life? What would you cling to that would be worth an eternity separated from God and loved ones - in hell? My life is a small price to pay for this treasure and like the one who "sold out" to get married, I haven't missed a thing. It has been my joy to sell out for Christ!

"Better is one day in your courts than a thousand elsewhere; I would rather be a doorkeeper in the house of my God than dwell in the tents of the wicked." (Psalm 84:10)

Dead Man Walking

Jesus said, **"For God so loved the world that he gave his one and only Son, that whoever believes in him shall not perish but have eternal life. For God did not send his Son into the world to condemn the world, but to save the world through him. Whoever believes in him is not condemned, but whoever does not believe stands condemned already because they have not believed in the name of God's one and only Son. This is the verdict: Light has come into the world, but people loved darkness instead of light because their deeds were evil. Everyone who does evil hates the light, and will not come into the light for fear that their deeds will be exposed. But whoever lives by the truth comes into the light, so that it may be seen plainly that what they have done has been done in the sight of God."** (John 3:16-21)

Bikers can be a pretty wild bunch. If you have any doubt, just check out Sturgis or Daytona after dark. There does, however, seem to be two kinds of bikers who get into trouble; those who have had a little too much beer and those who are hell bent on doing evil. At most bike events, we can anticipate that the booze will flow, bikes will smoke rubber and people will get a little nuts, but some will embrace anything just because it's evil.

I was walking down the sidewalk during a bike week in Galveston, Texas when I noticed a dozen men coming towards me, half walking and half running, stumbling over one another, all led by a single attractive woman. She seemed pretty enough, but these guys looked desperate; a pack of hungry hounds on the scent of a ham bone! As they came closer and then passed, I still didn't understand what was so special about this particular lady until someone pointed it out: she was topless! Naked from the waist up except for a very good paint job! It seems that local airbrush artists were spray painting "clothes" on willing women. This is typical of the wild and crazy stuff that happens at a motorcycle rally.

On another occasion, a very different group of men were coming towards me, this time led by nothing less than the angel of darkness himself. It was clear from what they were saying and the look in their eyes that they were on their way to hurt somebody. Their eyes were black and lifeless as their boots marched in rhythm, occasionally looking over their shoulders as if to see if they were being followed. This was something more than having a few too many beers or girl watching. This was evil on a mission and somebody was going to bleed.

As a pastor, I am often asked the same questions over and over again. One of them is, "Why would a good God send anyone to hell?" The answer is, "He doesn't." John 3:16-18 is possibly the best known, most frequently quoted and most memorized scripture of all time. It is also one of the most misunderstood.

These words of Jesus set the record straight: Sinners will not BE condemned one day. Rather, we ARE condemned from birth; all of us are born with a fatal disease commonly referred to as "sin." Sin destroys the eternal soul. The Gospel (meaning "good news") reads, "For God so loved the world that he gave his one and only Son, that whoever believes in him shall not perish but have eternal life." To further clarify, Jesus says, "God did not send his Son into the world to condemn the world, but to save the world through him" - and if that salvation is ignored or rejected, then we REMAIN condemned.

Would a terminal patient accuse a doctor who is bringing an antidote of coming to kill them? On the contrary! The doctor is actually bringing a cure or "good news." It is logical then, that someone who receives that antidote is no longer condemned to die but anyone refusing the help remains terminal. They are, as it were, already dead! God doesn't SEND anyone to hell. Those who end up there do so by stepping over the crucified body of Christ.

Jesus continues, "Light has come into the world, but people loved darkness instead of light…" Why does the world love darkness? Because the dark hides who we are and the bad things we do. Have you ever watched a couple of toddlers in a crib? At first they're just cooing and having fun, but it isn't long before one of them becomes bored, grabs a rattle from the other and bonks him over the head! The victim begins to cry, the assailant begins to cry and within moments we have chaos and anarchy in the nursery. Are babies evil? No, just human.

The difference between someone out to raise a little hell and someone out to do serious damage may be clarified by several theories including "Nature vs. Nurture." (Nature vs. Nurture asks the question, "Were they born that way or did they learn the behavior growing up?" The answer is "both!") In either case, there is certainly a correlation between time spent in the dark and inevitable behavior. The longer we linger in the dark and dance with the devil the greater the likelihood we will become lost there. It doesn't matter what we do (become jealous, get drunk, steal a bike or shoot someone in the head), the issue is the root of sin we were all born with. This sin will destroy you, but "…whoever lives by the truth comes into the light" and in the light we discover forgiveness and mercy, hope and peace. We once were condemned, but now we have been set free!

"Blessed is the one whose transgressions are forgiven, whose sins are covered. Blessed is the one whose sin the LORD does not count against them and in whose spirit is no deceit. When I kept silent, my bones wasted away through my groaning all day long. For day and night your hand was heavy on me; my strength was sapped as in the heat of summer. Then I acknowledged my sin to you and did not cover up my iniquity. I said, "I will confess my transgressions to the LORD." And you forgave the guilt of my sin. (Psalm 32:1-5)

Bad Reputation

[Jesus] came to a town in Samaria called Sychar, near the plot of ground Jacob had given to his son Joseph. Jacob's well was there, and Jesus, tired as he was from the journey, sat down by the well. It was about noon. When a Samaritan woman came to draw water, Jesus said to her, "Will you give me a drink?" (His disciples had gone into the town to buy food.) The Samaritan woman said to him, "You are a Jew and I am a Samaritan woman. How can you ask me for a drink?" (For Jews do not associate with Samaritans.) Jesus answered her, "If you knew the gift of God and who it is that asks you for a drink, you would have asked him and he would have given you living water." "Sir," the woman said, "you have nothing to draw with and the well is deep. Where can you get this living water? Are you greater than our father Jacob, who gave us the well and drank from it himself, as did also his sons and his livestock?" Jesus answered, "Everyone who drinks this water will be thirsty again, but whoever drinks the water I give them will never thirst. Indeed, the water I give them will become in them a spring of water welling up to eternal life." The woman said to him, "Sir, give me this water so that I won't get thirsty and have to keep coming here to draw water." He told her, "Go, call your husband and come back." "I have no husband," she replied. Jesus said to her, "You are right when you say you have no husband. The fact is, you have had five husbands, and the man you now have is not your husband. What you have just said is quite true."

"Sir," the woman said, "I can see that you are a prophet. Our ancestors worshiped on this mountain, but you Jews claim that the place where we must worship is in Jerusalem." "Woman," Jesus replied, "believe me, a time is coming when you will worship the Father neither on this mountain nor in Jerusalem. You Samaritans worship what you do not know; we worship what we do know, for salvation is from the Jews. Yet a time is coming and has now come when the true worshipers will worship the Father in the Spirit and in truth, for they are the kind of worshipers the Father seeks. God is spirit, and his worshipers must worship in the Spirit and in truth." The woman said, "I know that Messiah" (called Christ) "is coming. When he comes, he will explain everything to us." Then Jesus declared, "I, the one speaking to you—I am he." (John 4:1-26)

He was well over three hundred pounds, six feet and then some as he rolled into Reno's Street Vibrations late one afternoon. His body consumed that Road King as if he was riding a child's dirt bike. Long black greasy hair slipped out from beneath his novelty helmet and just sort of hung there; parts of it straight while some strands were clumped together in hopeless knots. His bandana was secured just above his dark sunglasses as if to give him a place to hide and his expression was something less that cheery. He wore a three piece embroidered patch on his back that doesn't need clarification for this story, but let's just say it contributed to peoples' perceived need to stare. Nobody seemed to know him, but on that street, on that day, he already had a bad reputation.

His menacing appearance was only partially responsible for the attention he was getting. It may have had a little something to do with the bright pink Harley-Davidson Road King he was riding. No stripes, no graphics – just solid PINK with a helmet to match! A smaller, less intimidating figure may have drawn a few snickers and winks, but nobody said a word or gave a clue that the color of his bike was anything out of the ordinary. Why? Because the patch on his back and the look on his face broadcasted a reputation that just wasn't worth messing with.

Reputations are funny things. While most people work hard to gain and maintain a good reputation, this biker was depending on his bad reputation to get him through. It might surprise you to know that Jesus was developing quite a bad reputation in the church of that day for breaking all kinds of religious and cultural rules. Sitting down and speaking with this Samaritan woman was a triple strike against Him. Respectable Jewish men were (1) not to speak with women in public, (2) not to associate with Samaritans (a despised ethnic people group of the day) and certainly (3) not to be seen with a woman whose own reputation had been soiled by no less than five previous relationships. But Jesus didn't care about reputations, He cared about people.

As He would often do, Jesus started with a simple question, "Will you give me a drink?" No preaching, no judgment, just a simple request for water because He was thirsty. The woman, however, was taken back by the obvious, "You are a Jew and I am a Samaritan woman. How can you ask me for a drink?" Jesus baits her; "If you knew who I was you would be asking me for a drink of water!" Not the kind of water that we drink which quenches our thirst for a little while – but spiritual water; the kind that keeps on satisfying, day after day, week after week, year after year, bringing our thirst for meaning and purpose to an end.

Jesus tells the woman to go and get her husband, knowing full well that she had no husband and was even now only living with a man. But He doesn't condemn her fornication; He just keeps presenting Himself as the answer to all of her questions and all of her deepest troubles. When she assures Jesus that she understands how one day a Messiah, a Savior will come, Jesus responds, "This is the day and I am the one."

Here we have two people, setting aside their reputations for just a moment, to get real. We all have less than spotless reputations, if not with people, certainly with God for He knows our every secret thought and motive. God knows, as do we, how much we are motivated by self-serving intentions. On the outside we might be a well-dressed, well spoken business person, but on the inside we are a desperately thirsty creature, looking for something…something we need but don't have. On the outside we might be a mountain of a man, menacing behind our sunglasses and leathers, but we're still as thirsty as any little boy coming in from play. We may have been married five times and now living with our most recent conquest, but we're still not satisfied, we're still not happy. We're strangely hungry, thirsty and in desperate need one way or another and Jesus is saying, "This is your day and I am the one." Jesus says, "Let anyone who is thirsty come to me and drink. Whoever believes in me, as Scripture has said, rivers of living water will flow from within them." (John 7:37-38)

"As the deer pants for streams of water, so my soul pants for you, my God. My soul thirsts for God, for the living God. When can I go and meet with God?" (Psalm 42:1-2)

No More Excuses

Now there is in Jerusalem near the Sheep Gate a pool, which in Aramaic is called Bethesda and which is surrounded by five covered colonnades. Here a great number of disabled people used to lie; the blind, the lame, the paralyzed. One who was there had been an invalid for thirty-eight years. When Jesus saw him lying there and learned that he had been in this condition for a long time, he asked him, "Do you want to get well?" "Sir," the invalid replied, "I have no one to help me into the pool when the water is stirred. While I am trying to get in, someone else goes down ahead of me." Then Jesus said to him, "Get up! Pick up your mat and walk." At once the man was cured; he picked up his mat and walked. (John 5:2-8)

How many times has someone approached you and your bike in a parking lot and said something like, "Man! She's beautiful! I'd love to have a motorcycle!" It happens to me almost weekly and I always ask the same question, "Then why don't you get one?" Now, I understand that some people may indeed have a valid reason for not buying a motorcycle, but the two most common answers I hear include: "My wife won't let me!" and "I can't afford it!"

To the first excuse I respond, "What, are you twelve years old?" Now before I lose half of my readers, let me assure you that I do understand and appreciate the fact that husbands and wives need to come together to discuss and work things out. I'm not suggesting that you surprise your spouse with a new motorcycle in the garage. (Please, I don't need the mail!) I believe instead, that we should love and respect one another by listening and submitting to one another. Perhaps one is concerned for their mate's safety and that is indeed a valid concern. Perhaps (as was our situation) the couple has small children and the wife wants to wait until the children are a little older before dad decides to risk his neck. But to simply dismiss any desire by blaming it on someone else is dishonest and unacceptable.

The second most common excuse for not buying a motorcycle is, "I can't afford it!" In many cases this is true. Even if you have the money you may have prioritized your funds for higher education or a home for your family. Maybe you feel that a private school is necessary for your children and a better investment. So often, however, it is a matter of other temporal priorities that keeps us from what we say we need or want.

One gentleman who lamented his inability to buy a motorcycle tried to guilt me with, "Gee! It must be nice to own a Harley-Davidson." My reply was, "Almost as nice as having a sports car, two horses and a speed boat like yours." More times than not, we do the things we really want to do and we make excuses for the rest. If you don't want a bike or prefer to have a summer place by the lake, don't blame it on your spouse or on the lack of funds. Put up or shut up!

People are like that! We make excuses rather than deal with the real issues. In this passage, Jesus walks up to a man who had been crippled for nearly forty years and asks, "Do you want to get well?" It's a simple question and the answer should have been immediate: "Yes! Yes! I want to get well!" Instead, he started listing all of the reasons why he couldn't: "No one will help me. Everyone keeps crowding me out." Jesus (and I love this!) completely ignores the man's excuses and tells him "Get up!" At that moment the crippled man had to make a decision to either stand or become a professional pool boy. I believe that if he had objected and continued on with his list of excuses Jesus may very well have walked on to the next person. Fortunately he chose to take God seriously and he walked away a free man.

I understand that it's not always that easy. Some people can't have or shouldn't spend money on a motorcycle. I understand that some people will never walk again or receive their sight, but if Jesus is asking, shouldn't we give it a try? The intent of this chapter is certainly not to encourage people to run out and buy material possessions – but to sit up and take notice when God speaks. Don't make excuses! Don't tell God why you can't do this or you can't do that! Shut up, get up and walk!

In many cases excuses have been bred into us: "You're stupid… you're worthless…you're not good for anything but digging ditches… you'll never amount to a hill of beans." We need, instead, to hear the voice of Jesus today who may be asking, "Do you want to walk? Do you want to change? Is there something you need?"

When we come to Christ, we must reject the curses of a former life and embrace the blessings that come with who we are, whose we are and what has been done for us! The Bible says, "…if anyone is in Christ, the new creation has come: The old has gone, the new is here!" (2 Corinthians 5:17)

That doesn't mean that we can have anything we want because some things would simply not be good for us and our Heavenly Father knows what is best. Neither does it suggest that we will never be sick or get injured, because life happens. What it does mean, however, is that we no longer have to sit by the pool and make excuses!

"When hard pressed, I cried to the LORD; he brought me into a spacious place. The LORD is with me; I will not be afraid. What can mere mortals do to me? The LORD is with me; he is my helper." (Psalm 118:5-7)

All Show And No Go

Jesus said, "When the Son of Man comes in his glory, and all the angels with him, he will sit on his glorious throne. All the nations will be gathered before him, and he will separate the people one from another as a shepherd separates the sheep from the goats. He will put the sheep on his right and the goats on his left.

Then the King will say to those on his right, 'Come, you who are blessed by my Father; take your inheritance, the kingdom prepared for you since the creation of the world. For I was hungry and you gave me something to eat, I was thirsty and you gave me something to drink, I was a stranger and you invited me in, I needed clothes and you clothed me, I was sick and you looked after me, I was in prison and you came to visit me.' Then the righteous will answer him, 'Lord, when did we see you hungry and feed you, or thirsty and give you something to drink? When did we see you a stranger and invite you in, or needing clothes and clothe you? When did we see you sick or in prison and go to visit you?' The King will reply, 'Truly I tell you, whatever you did for one of the least of these brothers and sisters of mine, you did for me.'

Then he will say to those on his left, 'Depart from me, you who are cursed, into the eternal fire prepared for the devil and his angels. For I was hungry and you gave me nothing to eat, I was thirsty and you gave me nothing to drink, I was a stranger and you did not invite me in, I needed clothes and you did not clothe me, I was sick and in prison and you did not look after me.' They also will answer, 'Lord, when did we see you hungry or thirsty or a stranger or needing clothes or sick or in prison, and did not help you?' He will reply, 'Truly I tell you, whatever you did not do for one of the least of these, you did not do for me.' Then they will go away to eternal punishment, but the righteous to eternal life." (Matthew 25:31-46)

Before I got into bikes I liked old cars - which turned out to be a lot more work than I had signed up for. The wife and I had a beautiful 1963 Ford Falcon convertible; black paint, black ragtop, red interior

79

and a red boot to cover the top when it was down. The wheels were stock spinners but also had red hubs and white walls. In the dash was a modern stereo made to look vintage so that we could keep the image but play our contemporary tunes as we rolled down Pacific Coast Highway. She was a looker, turning heads wherever we went!

Under the hood of that old Falcon was a nightmare; a tired straight six that had a difficult time getting out of its own way. Furthermore, that six banger was wired and duct taped to a worn out drive train and clunky transmission. She was as they say, "all show and no go!"

It wasn't long before I decided to get out of the old car game and buy a motorcycle. This time, I wasn't going to make the same mistake! My first bike was a late model Harley-Davidson Heritage Softail with only a few thousand miles. She ran like a clock and was easy on the eyes! As time went on, however, I continually added more chrome, giving little attention to performance and horsepower. She was a beautiful bike but my heart took a dip one afternoon when I heard the mechanic describe her as "all show and no go." She ran as good as any other stock motor, but I had not yet learned to appreciate what could be done to enhance her performance.

My two machines were perfect examples of what Jesus was talking about in this parable. Looks are one thing, but performance is another.

I must be cautious here: There is absolutely nothing that we can do to perform for God and thereby earn our salvation. Our salvation is absolutely free to us; a gift of God given through Jesus Christ. The second chapter of Ephesians makes this abundantly clear: "For it is by grace you have been saved, through faith—and this is not from yourselves, it is the gift of God—not by works, so that no one can boast." There is, however, a reasonable expectation that there will be evidence of God's changing power within us. John the Baptist told a group of religious snobs to "produce fruit in keeping with [their] repentance." (Matthew 3:8) Jesus repeatedly taught that we would be able to discern who the true followers of Christ were by looking at the fruit in their lives.

The fruit spoken of in this parable is giving food, drink, kindness and clothing to those who are in need. Kindness is also attributed to those who take the time to visit the sick and incarcerated. Jesus said, when you do these things for the "least of these" (the poor, the hungry, the needy) it is as if you were doing them for Christ Himself.

Let's consider for a moment how fruit is produced. Good fruit comes from healthy trees that have been watered, nurtured and bathed in just the right amount of sunlight. It simply makes sense that good trees will produce good fruit. What if, however, we were to take a sickly tree or better yet a plastic imitation tree and hang fruit on it? Would that be the same? Of course not! Hanging peaches on a thorn bush doesn't make it a peach tree any more than putting racing stripes on a six cylinder Falcon makes it a race car! Too many people calling themselves believers or even Christians are like a plastic tree or an old Ford Falcon. They look the part but they are all show and no go.

Jesus concludes with some frightening words in this parable. "Depart from me...into the eternal fire prepared for the devil and his angels." Someone will ask, "What if they HAD done more, given more and tried harder?" It would not have mattered. Listen to what

Jesus said to some who evidently DID do some amazing things in His name: "Many will say to me on that day, 'Lord, Lord, did we not prophesy in your name and in your name drive out demons and in your name perform many miracles?' Then I will tell them plainly, 'I never knew you. Away from me, you evildoers!'" (Matthew 7:22-23)

This impressive display of religious effort - even power, meant nothing to Jesus. The question is not, "Can you act like a Christian... can you look like a fruit tree...can you look like a race car?" The questions is, "Have you truly been changed (re-created) by the power of God, from the inside out, to perform in His name?" Furthermore, "Does the Holy Spirit live inside of you, producing the fruit of the Spirit?"

"...the fruit of the Spirit is love, joy, peace, [patience], kindness, goodness, faithfulness, gentleness and self-control. Against such things there is no law. Those who belong to Christ Jesus have crucified the flesh with its passions and desires. Since we live by the Spirit, let us keep in step with the Spirit." (Galatians 5:22-25) You've just got to ask yourself: "Am I the real deal or am I all show and no go?"

"One person gives freely, yet gains even more; another withholds unduly, but comes to poverty. A generous person will prosper; whoever refreshes others will be refreshed." (Proverbs 11:24-25)

The Best Wine

A wedding took place at Cana in Galilee. Jesus' mother was there, and Jesus and his disciples had also been invited to the wedding. When the wine was gone, Jesus' mother said to him, 'They have no more wine.' 'Woman, why do you involve me?' Jesus replied. 'My hour has not yet come.' His mother said to the servants, 'Do whatever he tells you.' Nearby stood six stone water jars, the kind used by the Jews for ceremonial washing, each holding from twenty to thirty gallons. Jesus said to the servants, 'Fill the jars with water'; so they filled them to the brim. Then he told them, 'Now draw some out and take it to the master of the banquet.' They did so, and the master of the banquet tasted the water that had been turned into wine. He did not realize where it had come from, though the servants who had drawn the water knew. Then he called the bridegroom aside and said, 'Everyone brings out the choice wine first and then the cheaper wine after the guests have had too much to drink; but you have saved the best till now.' What Jesus did here in Cana of Galilee was the first of the signs through which he revealed his glory; and his disciples believed in him. (John 2:1-11)

I chuckled as I read the t-shirt, "Ride! Eat! Repeat!" That sounded about right to me! Then there was the motto of one club that boasted, "When we meet, we eat!" Maybe it's the physical energy that it takes to handle a large v-twin or maybe it's just the fresh air. The bottom line is, you just cannot separate motorcycles from good food! One goes with the other.

Food makes everything better, doesn't it? And when the food runs out, it's time to go home! The World Series has hotdogs, while pizza is likely what you will find at a Super Bowl party. The state fair peddles funnel cake and fried Twinkies while no biker rally would be complete without barbecue and beer – and those great big turkey legs! In Jesus' time, however, the center of the party was the wine. Not because people wanted to get drunk, but because wine came with celebration! Water was the most common beverage, but for special occasions there needed to be good wine! All through the Old and New Testaments, wine symbolizes celebration and blessing and when the wine runs out, the party is over.

In this story, Jesus is still new on the scene. He has done no miracles yet and few people see Him as anyone special; let alone the Son of God. His mother, however, remembering God's promises before His birth, saw this night as an opportunity to introduce her amazing Son.

The wedding party had run out of wine, something that would have been a terrible embarrassment for the host and a disappointment for the guests. At first Jesus seems to object, but like so many mothers, Mary just kept talking and promoting her Son. After following His instructions, the wine was taken to the master of the banquet who was impressed with how good it was! Furthermore, he makes the point that most people put the good wine out first and save the lesser wine for those who have already had too much to drink. But in this case, the best wine had been saved for later in the party.

The fact that Jesus instantly turned one hundred and eighty gallons of water into wine is not such a big deal compared to some of His other miracles (blindness, leprosy and demon possession). What impresses me is that He would bother with such a trivial problem, and that this wine was of a particularly high quality. This should tell us two things about Jesus; that He cares about our day-to-day problems and that when He does something He does it right!

"He makes grass grow for the cattle, and plants for people to cultivate, bringing forth food from the earth: wine that gladdens human hearts, oil to make their faces shine, and bread that sustains their hearts." (Psalm 104:14-15)

Your Best Friend Ever

Jesus said, **"I am the good shepherd. The good shepherd lays down his life for the sheep. The hired hand is not the shepherd and does not own the sheep. So when he sees the wolf coming, he abandons the sheep and runs away. Then the wolf attacks the flock and scatters it. The man runs away because he is a hired hand and cares nothing for the sheep. I am the good shepherd; I know my sheep and my sheep know me just as the Father knows me and I know the Father—and I lay down my life for the sheep."** (John 10:11-15)

Bikers know people; a lot of people. We see one another at all the usual hangouts and rides and know them well enough to give them a nod or a hello. Then there are the people with whom we have ridden, not necessarily friends, but friendly. We've shared a burger with them, admired their bikes and gone our separate ways. Closer still, there are the two or three that are seen everywhere together; riding, eating, laughing and telling the same old road stories. You may even wear the same patch as they do on your back and know each other's families. You're friends, maybe even good friends, but they don't know your dreams, secrets and fears.

Some of us are fortunate enough to have a very best friend. You have crisscrossed the country together; explored every two-lane highway, greasy spoon and nasty motel. You have the memories and scars that tell the tales you will someday share with your grandchildren. You think nothing of riding side by side, for hundreds of miles at breakneck speeds because you know one another and have confidence in the other one's skill and ability to ride. You're more than friends, you're best friends. You would give this friend money or anything else they needed without a second thought. You would fight to defend them and even die for them if necessary. Best friends have the right to tell each other when one of them is acting like a jerk and needs to straighten up – because you have their back and they have yours. They truly are a "brother" or a "sister."

Jesus explains here, in a first century agrarian culture, that there are two kinds of shepherds; those who are invested in the sheep and those who have been hired to do a job. If a shepherd owns his sheep he has come to know them well. A flock of sheep will recognize the sound of their master's voice and come to him when called. In turn, shepherds will often name the members of their flock, likely after a unique marking, a personality or physical defect. "That one over there is ol' Grouchy. The one on the hill is One Eyed Pete and this little guy I call Peewee." There is such a connection with his animals that even if a wild beast were to challenge the shepherd, he would defend them with his life!

Compare that sense of love and responsibility to someone who has been hired for the day or the week to watch the sheep. They are paid a minimum wage to do what they believe is a menial job. All goes well until trouble comes. If a thief or a wolf happens upon them, the hired servant will quickly abandon the sheep and run for his life.

Jesus tells us (i.e. the sheep) that He is indeed the "Good Shepherd." He's not just one of the better shepherds, but THE shepherd. He knows us by name. He knows who we are, what we are like, our personality, character flaws, talents and abilities, likes and dislikes and even our physical limitations and internal concerns. Jesus knows us inside and out and yet He says, "I lay down my life for [you]."

There is an Old Testament proverb that reads: "One who has unreliable friends soon comes to ruin, but there is a friend who sticks closer than a brother." (Proverbs 18:24) Jesus, in speaking with His twelve closest friends said, "I no longer call you servants, because a servant does not know his master's business. Instead, I have called you friends, for everything that I learned from my Father I have made known to you." (John 15:15) Jesus also said, "Greater love has no one than this: to lay down one's life for one's friends." And lay down His life He certainly did when He was nailed to a cross, a sacrifice on our behalf, a payment for our sins. Our friend, our very BEST friend, picked up the tab for every evil thing we have ever done, every evil thought we have ever had. He doesn't just "have our back", He purchased our eternal souls with His own blood, giving us the gift of eternal life. What better friend do you have than that?

Friendship goes both ways, you know! I ride with you and you ride with me. I've got your back and you've got mine. That's just the way friendship is; two people looking out for the other's best interest. That's why Jesus said, "You are my friends if you do what I command." (John 15:14) We understand that friends don't generally "command" one another, but we're talking about God here. He's the biggest kid on the block and He considers us friends. We would be wise to listen and do whatever He says.

"A friend loves at all times, and a brother is born for a time of adversity." (Proverbs 17:17)

Posers On The Road

Jesus said, **"A man was going down from Jerusalem to Jericho, when he was attacked by robbers. They stripped him of his clothes, beat him and went away, leaving him half dead. A priest happened to be going down the same road, and when he saw the man, he passed by on the other side. So too, a Levite, when he came to the place and saw him, passed by on the other side. But a Samaritan, as he traveled, came where the man was; and when he saw him, he took pity on him. He went to him and bandaged his wounds, pouring on oil and wine. Then he put the man on his own donkey, brought him to an inn and took care of him. The next day he took out two denarii and gave them to the innkeeper. 'Look after him,' he said, 'and when I return, I will reimburse you for any extra expense you may have.'"** (Luke 10:30-35)

There are few things more annoying than a poser; someone who pretends to be one thing but is actually something else. Posers dress the part and have memorized all of the right things to say. They look and sound good, but they are, in reality, phonies!

The story is told of a biker who stopped in front of a church one Sunday, parked his bike and went in to worship. The pastor, surprised by the man's appearance of long hair, leather jacket, piercings and tattoos suggested that the man leave immediately and come back when he had considered how Jesus would dress if he were to come to this church. The following week the biker returned to the church dressed as he had been the week before. Once again, the preacher approached the visitor, asking him if he had asked Jesus how He would dress if He were to come to this church. The biker responded, "Jesus said He would never come to a church like this one."

God does not live in a suit of clothes. He lives in the hearts of people. Adolf Hitler was a well-dressed, clean cut and clean-shaven man. So were John Dillinger and Al Capone. What does that prove?

The priest and Levite in this story were well-educated, religious people, no doubt well dressed and groomed, but they had no time to help the victim of a brutal mugging, left in a ditch to die. Later that same day a Samaritan came along; an ethnic outcast scorned by the Jewish elite of the day. He may not have had the right clothes or pedigree, but he did have a good heart, the time and a little bit of money to give his injured neighbor. Jesus uses this parable to scold the pretenders that look good on the outside and know all of the right words, but possess hearts that are selfish and indifferent.

The message of the Gospel is that we are sinners and there isn't anything we ourselves can do about it. We are out of touch with God and have no hope of making peace with Him. We can clean up, dress up and shape up but we are still sinners separated from a Holy God. But God, in all of His love and mercy, through the sacrifice of Jesus Christ on the cross, re-creates us from the inside out! It's truly a regenerative miracle! The scriptures actually call us a "new creation." (2 Corinthians 5:17) As sinners we are "dead men walking." People acting religiously are corpses who have been washed and dressed in a new set of clothes and propped up in the corner. Real Christians, however, have been re-created from the inside out; born again!

Many people (like the pastor in this story), think that people must clean themselves up before coming to God. They must quit smoking, quit drinking and quit cussing. And since we're not very good at giving up these sorts of things we simply feel unworthy to darken the door of a church. Many times I have heard someone say, "If I were to come to your church the roof would fall in!" But the Bible says that, "While we were STILL sinners, Christ died for us!" (Romans 5:8) God did not reach out to us AFTER we cleaned ourselves up – but during our worst state of being.

To avoid being a poser, come to Christ just as you are. Confess your sins and grow a little bit each day. Read God's Word and do what it says. Then find a church that has a parking space for your bike and doesn't mind the way you look or dress.

"Have mercy on me, O God, according to your unfailing love; according to your great compassion blot out my transgressions. Wash away all my iniquity and cleanse me from my sin." (Psalm 51:1-2)

Bad Company

While Jesus was having dinner at Matthew's house, many tax collectors and sinners came and ate with him and his disciples. When the Pharisees saw this, they asked his disciples, "Why does your teacher eat with tax collectors and sinners?" On hearing this, Jesus said, "It is not the healthy who need a doctor, but the sick. But go and learn what this means: 'I desire mercy, not sacrifice.' For I have not come to call the righteous, but sinners." (Matthew 9:10-13)

Our local Harley-Davidson dealership donates hot-dogs, hamburgers and sodas to their HOG chapter, who in turn hosts a weekly drop-in barbecue for all riders. It's a quick and easy lunch for those passing by and it raises money for all the good causes supported by the Harley Owners Group. People come and go, sit and chat and have a good time hanging out with friends.

I had been riding less than a year when I stopped by for lunch one day and a gentleman that I knew passed by and slapped me on the shoulder saying, "Hi Pastor Marty! How ya' doing?" Until that point I had not noticed the crusty old guy at the end of my table. His hair was gray, his skin was weathered and his beard was limited to short stubble. When he heard my friend refer to me as a pastor he dropped what he was reading and inquired quite loudly, "Pastor? What the hell is a pastor doing at a Harley shop?" I smiled and answered, "Pastors have to eat too." With that, he got up out of his chair and walked over to me, plopping a Playboy magazine in front of me, centerfold showing. "Well pastor, what do you think of these?" he asked with a sinister chuckle. I kept my cool and replied, "God is an amazing Creator, isn't He?" At first, the old biker just glared at me but within seconds he was laughing hard and slapping me on the back, causing me to spill my soda. I made a new friend that day.

There are those who would have rather me be offended and express my indignation. Why would I have done that? In the first place, that's exactly what this old coot wanted me to do; get mad and stomp away, proving that Christians are somehow made of glass and out of touch. Secondly, this man was acting predictably. I would have been shocked indeed if one of my Christian brothers had shown me the Playboy, but this was an old school biker just doing what he does; acting crude and seeing if he could get a reaction. But most importantly, by not losing my cool, a door of communication was opened that has not been shut to this very day.

Years later I had the privilege of performing this man's wedding; not his first I am sure. On several occasions, I was able to pray with him before a ride. I am convinced that I was right where Jesus would have been on that day; meeting people and eating with sinners.

Let's first make this point: we are ALL sinners! The Bible tells us in several places, "All have sinned and fallen short of the glory of God." (Romans 3:23) Some lie, some cheat and some steal. Some are very colorful and creative in their sinning (bikers, movie stars and musicians come to mind) while others sit behind closed doors and keep their sins a secret. Jesus told us that hating someone is the same as murder and that lusting after a beautiful woman is committing adultery in our hearts. (Matthew 5:27) Some sin small and some sin big, but sin is sin and it's that seed within us that separates us from God and creates our need for a Savior.

Jesus often met and ate with sinners and the highly religious people of the day didn't like it. They seemed to think that those with the medicine shouldn't be seen in the company of those who are sick. They were more concerned about what other religious people might say than loving and caring for those in need. Pharisees would never miss a sacrifice, break a law (many of which they had invented themselves) or put themselves in the proximity of tax collectors, lepers or whores, but Jesus indicated He is far more interested in mercy than in religious rituals.

Jesus Christ, the Son of God, was holy and sinless, but He was no stick in the mud. We can imagine that there were some off color jokes that day at Matthew's house and maybe even a few women whose reputations had been tarnished. Jesus, however, the Great Physician, was right where He belonged and doing what He had come to do. He was a light in the darkness, a breath of fresh air and a monolith of hope for the hopeless. Jesus loved people; sinners and saints alike. He did not condone their sin but forgave them and instructed them to "go and sin no more." (John 8:11) Jesus loves sinners just the way they are, but too much to leave them that way.

Those of us in motorcycle ministry walk a line; directed by God to live a life worthy of our calling. But we are also commanded to go into the world and preach the Gospel. I welcome, therefore, the opportunity to occasionally keep bad company - if only to be a friend and remind others that someone came to die for their sins.

"Good and upright is the LORD; therefore he instructs sinners in his ways. He guides the humble in what is right and teaches them his way." (Psalm 25:8-9)

How Should I Know?

As [Jesus] went along, he saw a man blind from birth. His disciples asked him, "Rabbi, who sinned, this man or his parents, that he was born blind?" "Neither this man nor his parents sinned," said Jesus, "but this happened so that the works of God might be displayed in him."

After saying this, he spit on the ground, made some mud with the saliva, and put it on the man's eyes. "Go," he told him, "wash in the Pool of Siloam" (this word means 'sent'). So the man went and washed, and came home seeing. His neighbors and those who had formerly seen him begging asked, "Isn't this the same man who used to sit and beg?" Some claimed that he was. Others said, "No, he only looks like him." But he himself insisted, "I am the man." "How then were your eyes opened?" they asked. He replied, "The man they call Jesus made some mud and put it on my eyes. He told me to go to Siloam and wash. So I went and washed, and then I could see." "Where is this man?" they asked him. "I don't know," he said.

They brought to the Pharisees the man who had been blind. Now the day on which Jesus had made the mud and opened the man's eyes was a Sabbath. Therefore the Pharisees also asked him how he had received his sight. "He put mud on my eyes," the man replied, "and I washed, and now I see." Some of the Pharisees said, "This man is not from God, for he does not keep the Sabbath." But others asked, "How can a sinner perform such signs?" So they were divided. Then they turned again to the blind man, "What have you to say about him? It was your eyes he opened." The man replied, "He is a prophet." They still did not believe that he had been blind and had received his sight until they sent for the man's parents. "Is this your son?" they asked. "Is this the one you say was born blind? How is it that now he can see?" "We know he is our son," the parents answered, "and we know he was born blind. But how he can see now, or who opened his eyes, we don't know. Ask him. He is of age; he will speak for himself." His parents said this because they were afraid of the Jewish leaders, who already had decided that anyone who acknowledged that Jesus was the Messiah would be put out of the synagogue. That was why his parents said, "He is of age; ask him." A second time they summoned the man who had been blind. "Give glory to God by telling the truth," they said. "We know this man is a sinner." He replied, "Whether he is a sinner or not, I don't know. One thing I do know. I was blind but now I see!" (John 9:1-3, 6-25)

I love Harley-Davidson motorcycles and so do most of my friends! The phrase, "Rolling Art" describes them well. I am fascinated by the lines, the curves and the attention given to every detail. I enjoy the various combinations of paint colors and chrome and leather seats. I love the way every rider customizes their bike, even if just a little bit, to make it uniquely their own. I never tire of looking at Harley books or even walking through the parking lot at events. The bikes remind me of lollipops lined up in a row, just waiting to be chosen for a ride.

When I'm done looking at Harley-Davidsons, I like reading about them and their history. I had the privilege of visiting the Harley-Davidson Museum in Milwaukee last summer. That was cool! I wore a headset which allowed me to hear the stories behind each exhibit and so many of the photos. Furthermore, I appreciate the Americana that each motorcycle represents. While I was disappointed to learn that Harleys are no longer made 100% in the United States, they still are for the most part and are celebrating well over a hundred years of design and innovation. I'm hooked! I'm a true fan! What else can I say?

Ask me how a Harley works and I wouldn't have a clue! The combustion engine has been painstakingly explained to me on more than a few occasions and I still don't know the difference between a muffler bearing and a canuder valve. But it doesn't hinder my absolute love and appreciation for a Heritage Softail Classic one little bit. I love the way they sound (especially with straight fishtails) and I love the way they make me feel when I'm rolling down the road, but I have no idea what makes them go "potato potato potato."

The poor man in this story was born blind from birth and I think we can assume he was no Helen Keller. In that day a blind man was not educated. There were no such things as schools for the blind, seeing eye dogs or even brail. His job was to go and sit in the streets and beg for money so that he could live. Then Jesus comes along and heals him in such a way that even our modern doctors would not be able to explain; spitting in the dirt and rubbing the mud in his eyes. The bewildered man then runs off to wash his eyes and when he does, HE CAN SEE! For the first time in maybe twenty or thirty years, HE CAN SEE!

First he sees his own reflection in the water, but he may not know that it's him. Later he sees his friends AND HIS PARENTS for the very first time! He runs and jumps and people are struggling to believe that this really is that blind man who once sat on the corner begging for change. He's smiling and laughing and talking a mile a minute - but he cannot explain what happened.

Such a dramatic miracle caused plenty of unwanted attention and was difficult for the Pharisees to dismiss. The religious elite of the day were not happy because all of this commotion only further validated this man Jesus whom they were already beginning to hate. They went to the man who was healed and even to his parents to ask them a barrage of questions that they either could not or would not answer. In the end, we can hear the exasperation of the newly sighted man when he says, "One thing I do know. I was blind but now I see!"

There are billions of Christians around the world; people who have experienced God through His Son Jesus Christ. Some have been saved out of alcoholism and drug addiction while others have had marriages and families restored. In spite of some flashy evangelists and outright charlatans, tens of thousands will assure you that they have been healed by the power of God and nothing anyone says will convince them otherwise.

In each case we could ask, "How did it work?" and I am sure that the honest ones would say, "I don't know!" How were they delivered from substance abuse? How were their families reunited? How was that stage four cancer patient suddenly declared cancer free? I don't know and neither do they. We don't have any more of an idea today than they did in Jesus' day. The good news is that we don't have to know. We don't have to explain anything! All we have to do is say, "Thank-you Jesus" and enjoy the ride home.

The Lord asks: **"Who is this that obscures my plans with words without knowledge? Brace yourself like a man; I will question you, and you shall answer me. Where were you when I laid the earth's foundation? Tell me, if you understand. Who marked off its dimensions? Surely you know! Who stretched a measuring line across it? On what were its footings set, or who laid its cornerstone while the morning stars sang together and all the angels shouted for joy? Who shut up the sea behind doors when it burst forth from the womb, when I made the clouds its garment and wrapped it in thick darkness, when I fixed limits for it and set its doors and bars in place, when I said, 'This far you may come and no farther; here is where your proud waves halt?' Have you ever given orders to the morning, or shown the dawn its place, that it might take the earth by the edges and shake the wicked out of it? The earth takes shape like clay under a seal; its features stand out like those of a garment.**
Have you journeyed to the springs of the sea or walked in the recesses of the deep? Have the gates of death been shown to you? Have you seen the gates of the deepest darkness? Have you comprehended the vast expanses of the earth? Tell me, if you know all this." (Job 38:2-18)

Hard Core

Jesus said to His followers, **"Truly I tell you, unless you eat the flesh of the Son of Man and drink his blood, you have no life in you. Whoever eats my flesh and drinks my blood has eternal life, and I will raise them up at the last day. For my flesh is real food and my blood is real drink. Whoever eats my flesh and drinks my blood remains in me, and I in them.**
On hearing it, many of his disciples said, "This is a hard teaching. Who can accept it?" ...From this time many of his disciples turned back and no longer followed him. (John 6:53-56 and 60 and 66)

I respect all bikers. I'm not one of those who won't give "the wave" to someone because they are riding the wrong brand of motorcycle. I believe it's not a matter of WHAT you ride but THAT you ride that earns you my respect. Together we dodge the cages, lobby for rider's rights and share the same road on two wheels. We are all riders! 'Nuff said!

I also understand that riding means something different to each person. At one end of the spectrum we have **the commuter**; a person who doesn't care so much about motorcycles as he does an economical means of transportation. This rider uses a lot of bungee cords, rides to work sporting a bright orange vest and wears booties to cover his Florsheim loafers (the kind with the little tassels!). He may or may not enjoy the ride but would trade his motorcycle in a New York minute for a BMW convertible - if the price of gas would just go down.

Next, we have **the week-end warrior** or RUB (which stands for Rich Urban Biker); someone who genuinely loves motorcycles, dressing up on the weekends for a medium distance ride, a burger and perhaps a beer. RUBs have the most chrome and the fewest miles on their bikes. Their haircuts and piercings are limited because they have to be back at the office on Monday morning where they will work very hard to pay for all of that shiny stuff on their motorcycle!

Hard core bikers are few and in a class all by themselves. It's not just a motorcycle, it's a lifestyle. Where they live, what they do and who they live with all must conform to the reality that they are bikers. If necessary, their scoot is parked in the living room next to the television. Mess with their bike (which is probably black) and you're going to get hurt.

They don't wear leather because it's fashionable, but because they have been down and they know how much it hurts. They wear blue jeans, engineer boots and tee shirts that say things like, "Ride til' You Die" and "Choppers for Life." (Note: RUBs wear those same shirts but they're just kidding!) Hard core bikers eat, sleep and live motorcycles. Everything else is secondary.

I know that right now many of you reading this are either disagreeing with my definitions or are trying to assess where you fit in. It's not a perfect scale but rather an attempt to put the words "hard core" in perspective.

There is no doubt that Jesus was a hardcore individual on a brutally unpopular and dangerous mission. He came knowing that He would die a horrible death on a Roman cross; first beaten beyond recognition and then nailed through the feet and hands to a piece of wood which was lifted up and dropped into the ground. The scriptures foretold it. He was no martyr who had His life taken from Him! He was a willing sacrifice that marched to the cross, crawled up on it and died for the sins of the world. Jesus was no wimp! No wannabe! No poser! He was the real deal doing what needed to be done.

Jesus calls His disciples to be hardcore and fully committed as well. In fact, history tells us that eleven of his twelve closest friends died horrible and violent deaths. They were stoned, crucified, boiled in oil and torn apart by wild animals. We're not likely to endure such a fate in twenty-first century America, but we have still been called as disciples to live sacrificially for Christ and die daily to our own ambitions and will.

Much like my description of riders, Jesus could have put His followers on a continuum as well. There were those who showed up just to watch and get free miracles and there were those who followed at a distance – whenever the conditions were right. The scriptures speak of the "one hundred and twenty" who followed Jesus as well as the "seventy" who were sent out as missionaries. Most people know about the "twelve" disciples who went almost everywhere with Jesus but upon closer examination we see that there were indeed "three" who were exceptionally close to the Master: Peter, James and John. Even still, in the end and at the cross there was only John, the beloved, described as "the one whom Jesus loved." Identifying with Jesus in front of the Roman guards was certainly an extreme and dangerous act indeed.

In this sixth chapter of the Gospel of John, Jesus chooses graphic words and images to describe Himself; almost as if to discourage lukewarm followers. But Jesus was not promoting cannibalism when He said "…unless you eat the flesh of the Son of Man and drink his blood, you have no life in you." As usual Jesus was speaking in metaphors and allegory, referring to Himself as the bread of life, living water, the sheep gate and the true vine. As with the flesh and blood, these too we understand to be descriptive and not literal. What Jesus was saying was, there are those who will follow me and there are those who will ingest me, not literally but figuratively. Jesus was saying that we must do far more than simply follow Him. It's not even enough to be followers or mere believers for thousands followed Jesus and even the devil is said to believe. So what? We must take Christ and all that He is and all that He has said and bring Him fully into our inner most being if we want to become hard core disciples. Was Jesus too radical, too extreme, too graphic? Evidently, because the Bible tells us, "From this time many of his disciples turned back and no longer followed him."

Jesus had asked, "Does this [talk] offend you?" I can almost hear Him say, "Then what will you do when things REALLY become difficult?" The teachings of Jesus Christ were more radical and revolutionary than anyone before or ever since! He said "crazy" things like "love your enemies" and "lose your life to save it." He offended the religious leaders of His day when He embraced lepers, ate with sinners and forgave prostitutes. If you would be His follower today you would be compelled to believe that He was and is God Almighty, the Creator of the universe, the One who raises the dead as He Himself was raised. (Wait! Think about that for just a moment. Jesus was dead – and was then raised from death by the power of God! Can you accept that?) To be His disciple you would need to put Him first in everything you do and expect His immanent return! (Yes! We believe Jesus is coming back!)

Some people are socially religious while others are quite serious about their faith. Still others are hardcore, selling their possessions and moving to a third world country where they serve the poorest of the poor; bringing them a means to live better and telling them about Jesus. If you're just looking for something to do on Sunday mornings don't go to church, go for a motorcycle ride or take up golf! But if you're looking for someone who is worthy of your every minute, your every dollar and your every breath – follow Jesus! Surrender your whole heart to Him! Take all that He is, all that He has and all that He has to offer and devour Him piece by piece! In other words, make

Him part of who you are! Feast upon His goodness, His love and His mercy. If you're going to be hardcore, do it for someone worthy of the sacrifice!

An Old Testament prophecy, speaking of Jesus says: **"Surely he took up our pain and bore our suffering, yet we considered him punished by God, stricken by him, and afflicted. But he was pierced for our transgressions, he was crushed for our iniquities; the punishment that brought us peace was on him, and by his wounds we are healed. We all, like sheep, have gone astray, each of us has turned to our own way; and the LORD has laid on him the iniquity of us all. He was oppressed and afflicted, yet he did not open his mouth; he was led like a lamb to the slaughter, and as a sheep before its shearers is silent, so he did not open his mouth."** (Isaiah 53:4-7)

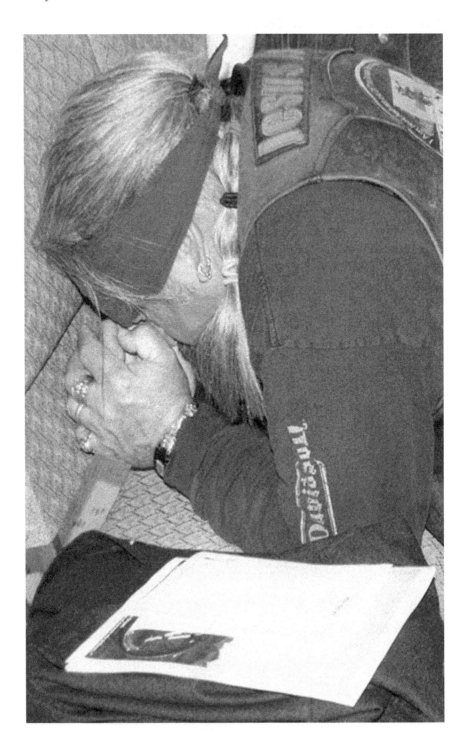

EPILOGUE
How To Become a Christian

You have just finished reading a few stories and parables told by Jesus Christ in the New Testament. It doesn't matter that we were not able to include all of them, for in the Gospel of John it tells us, "Jesus performed many other signs in the presence of his disciples, which are not recorded in this book. **But these are written that you may believe that Jesus is the Messiah, the Son of God**, and that by believing you may have life in his name." (John 20:30-31)

If you snicker at the prospect of a biker giving their life to Christ, then we'll just keep praying for you and all of those who ride. We love and respect you and will continue to celebrate our mutual passion for motorcycles. If, however, you are interested, curious or willing to explore further, consider the scriptures below as an explanation for why we need a Savior and how to become a follower of Christ.

The Book of Romans is a letter sent from Paul, an Apostle in the early church to the Christians in Rome, Italy. In this book, Paul explains in great detail the claims of Christ and our need to respond to Him as God. A selected series of scriptures have been tagged, "The Romans Road" and are an effective and simple way of explaining the Gospel.

In Romans 3:23, (that is, chapter three and verse twenty-three) we read, **"For all have sinned, and come short of the glory of God."** We have all sinned. Everybody who has ever lived, the good and the bad, preachers and politicians have sinned. If we are honest with ourselves this is not too difficult of a concept to accept. Romans 3:10-18 continues with a detailed picture of what sin looks like in our lives. But remember: It doesn't matter what sins we have committed (big or small). It's the fact that we are all guilty of sin.

Next we read Romans 6:23, which teaches us about the consequences of our sin - **"For the wages of sin is death; but the gift of God is eternal life through Jesus Christ our Lord."** The punishment that we will receive for our sin is death. Not just physical death, but eternal death! But don't be fearful or discouraged! Romans 6:23 continues: **"but the gift of God is eternal life through Jesus Christ our Lord."** Yes, we are sinners and therefore estranged from God, but God knows that! And knowing that we are powerless to simply stop sinning, He sent His son in the form of a baby to live a sinless life and then die as a sacrifice for our sins on the cross! (John 3:16 reads: **"For God so loved the world that he gave his one and only Son, that whoever believes in him shall not perish but have eternal life."**)

I really appreciate Romans 5:8 which dispels the myth that we need to clean ourselves up before coming to God; that we need to "straighten up and fly right" and get our lives in order. The truth of the matter is, **"God demonstrates his own love toward us, in that while we were still sinners, Christ died for us."** (Romans 5:8) Isn't that beautiful? Jesus loves you just the way you are!

Mom and dad, think about this for a moment: Do you love your children when they come in from play, covered in dirt, sweaty and smelly? Sure you do! You accept their hugs and kisses – and then you throw them in the bathtub! God loves us just the way we are, but He loves us too much to leave us that way.

People are often concerned that when they come to Christ they will have to give up all of those things they think they love and need. Allow me another illustration from "Parenting 101." You're at the zoo and your child is licking away on a fudgesicle when he drops it on the ground. It's now covered in dirt, human traffic and animal hair. But when you attempt to take the fudgesicle away you know what happens! That kid clings to his frozen furry delight with both hands, screaming his lunges out. If he were mature enough to trust you he would realize that you are more than willing to replace that filthy mess with another fudgesicle or something even better. Good parents look out for their children and strive to give them the very best. Keep in mind that your father in heaven is no different. Jesus said, **"If you, then, though you are evil, know how to give good gifts to your children, how much more will your Father in heaven give good gifts to those who ask him!"** (Matthew 7:11) God loves you just the way you are, but he has so much more in store for you!

Our next stop on the Romans road is Romans 10:9. **"If you confess with your mouth Jesus as Lord, and believe in your heart that God raised Him from the dead, you will be saved."** Romans 10:13 says it again, **"for everyone who calls on the name of the Lord will be saved."** Jesus died as a sacrifice for our sins. He has paid the price – there is nothing left for us to do except trust in His ability to save us. Salvation and the forgiveness of sins, is available to anyone who will surrender their life to Jesus Christ, our Lord and Savior.

The result of our decision to come to Christ is captured in Romans

5:1 where it says, **"Therefore, since we have been justified through faith, we have peace with God through our Lord Jesus Christ."** This may take some time for you to comprehend. YOU HAVE BEEN FORGIVEN! God forgives you even if you struggle to forgive yourself! Be encouraged by Romans 8:1 which tells us, **"Therefore, there is now no condemnation for those who are in Christ Jesus."** Isn't that great? Because of Jesus we will never be condemned for our sins! You may think, "Well, that's not fair! I deserve to be punished for my sins!" And you are absolutely correct! We do indeed deserve to be punished, but God has a better way. It's called "grace." Grace is getting something far better that what we deserve! **"For it is by grace you have been saved, through faith—and this is not from yourselves, it is the gift of God— not by works, so that no one can boast."** (Ephesians 2:8-9) I heard one pastor describe grace as "God's riches at Christ's expense!" or "G.R.A.C.E." Any way that you look at it, it's just too precious of a gift to ignore or pass up.

Are you ready to give your heart to God? Are you ready to ask Jesus into your heart and life? Read again the scripture verses above and then pray this prayer. There is no magic in just saying these words, but if you pray them sincerely from your heart, God will listen.

"Dear God, I know that I have sinned against you and am deserving of death. But Jesus took the punishment that I deserve so that through faith in Him I could be forgiven. With your help, I place my trust in you for my salvation. I surrender my life to you right now! Thank you for your wonderful grace and forgiveness, and the gift of eternal life! Amen!"

There's more good news! Romans 8:38-39 says, **"For I am convinced**

that neither death nor life, neither angels nor demons, neither the present nor the future, nor any powers, neither height nor depth, nor anything else in all creation, will be able to separate us from the love of God that is in Christ Jesus our Lord." Some days you may become discouraged or doubtful, but God won't let go of you – ever! You might not "feel" saved or "feel" like a Christian, but it doesn't depend on you or your feelings – it depends on God! He will be faithful when you are not. He will love you when you can't love yourself. God has said, **"I have loved you with an everlasting love; I have drawn you with unfailing kindness."** (Jeremiah 31:3)

Now That You Believe

Every seedling needs to be planted in good soil, fertilized, watered carefully and receive just the right amount of sunlight. Likewise, every newborn baby needs to be kept warm, fed the right foods and loved. As a new Christian, you will want to do everything possible to nurture and encourage your new faith. Here is a short list for growing with Christ.

1. **Tell someone what you have decided!** If you know someone who is a Christian, give them a call right now! There's something very powerful about "saying the words" and "confessing" Christ. Telling someone else about your decision will not only encourage you, it will encourage them as well. If you don't have anyone that you can go to, contact our offices at www.BlackSheepHDFC.org We'd love to hear your story!

2. **Find a good Christian church where you feel comfortable.** There are likely dozens of Christian churches within a few miles of where you live. The "style" of the church is not important. Some are very formal while others are relaxed. The way people dress and the music that is played will vary. You'll want to find a church in which you feel comfortable. Ask God to direct you to the best church for you. If you have any questions about finding a church home, you are always welcome to contact us at www.BlackSheepHDFC.org

2. **Start reading the Bible.** All of the scriptures in this book came from the New International version of the Bible. We would encourage

you to NOT start reading in Genesis, the first book of the Bible. (This can be pretty advanced for a new Christian.) Begin by reading through the Gospel of John and then maybe the Gospel of Luke. Become familiar with the teachings of Jesus. As you grow, attending church and perhaps a Bible study, you will find your way into the other books of the Bible. It's not important how much you read, but that you take the time to read everyday and absorb what you read. When you don't understand something, write it down and don't be afraid the ask questions. It's how we learn.

3. **Pray every day and throughout the day.** Prayer is simply talking to God. If you will compare it to talking with a spouse or a close friend you will understand that there are times when you "chat" and there are times when you need to go nose to nose. We would encourage you to chat with God constantly! Ask Him questions. Tell Him how you feel. When you wake up in the morning say a prayer before your feet touch the ground. Something like, "Dear God, here I go! Please go with me and guide me throughout the day." Talk with Him as you ride and drive (remembering to keep your eyes open at all times!). There will, however, be those other times – daily times, when you sit down and read your Bible and need to have an extended "nose to nose" with God. These times should include **confessing** your sins, **asking Him for what you need** and **thanking Him for all that He** has done for you.

4. **Find some new friends.** We're not suggesting that you abandon all of your old friends, unless of course they are a source of serious temptation for you. You will soon learn that God's family is like every other family in that we're not perfect. People will disappoint you but God never will. Keep your eyes on Jesus! It will be helpful, however,

for you to find some new riding buddies who share your same faith and desire to follow God.

God bless you and keep you as you for Jesus!

CPSIA information can be obtained
at www.ICGtesting.com
Printed in the USA
FSHW010200291121

9 781456 752354